SEVERN WAY OFFICIAL WALKERS' GUIDE

Introduction to the Severn Way	2
Countryside Codes	5
Planning the Walk	6
The Route of the Severn Way	9
Rhyd-y-benwch to the Source	10
The Source to Old Hall (Neuadd)	12
Old Hall (Neuadd) to Llanidloes	14
Llanidloes	16
Llanidloes to Waen	18
Waen to Cefn-coch	20
Cefn-coch to Newtown	22
Newtown to Brynderwen	24
Brynderwen to Llwynderw	26
Llwynderw to Pool Quay	28
Pool Quay to Llandrinio	30
Llandrinio to Wilcott	32
Wilcott to Montford Bridge	34
Montford Bridge to Shrewsbury	36
Shrewsbury	38
Shrewsbury to Atcham	40
Atcham to Cressage	42
Cressage to Ironbridge	44
Ironbridge to Apley Forge	46
Apley Forge to Bridgnorth	48
Bridgnorth	50
Bridgnorth to Hampton (Ferry)	52

Ham	
Uppe	
Bewd	
Bewd	
Shrawley Wood to Camp House Inn	62
Camp House Inn to Diglis Locks	64
Worcester	66
Diglis Locks to Clifton	68
Clifton to Holdfast	70
Holdfast to Tewkesbury Park	72
Tewkesbury	74
Tewkesbury Park to Wainlode	76
Wainlode to Walham	78
Walham to Wicksgreen	80
Gloucester	82
Wicksgreen to Upper Framilode	84
Upper Framilode to Frampton	86
Frampton to Slimbridge	88
Slimbridge to Newtown	90
Newtown to Shepperdine	92
Shepperdine to Littleton	94
Littleton to Severn Beach	96
Severn Beach to Sea Mills	98
Sea Mills to Bristol	100
Useful Contacts	102
Acknowledgememts	103

C000204104

A walk along the length of the Severn is a geography lesson brought vividly to life, every step helping to put flesh on the bare bones of what we all learn at school about the stages of a river's journey as it progresses from source to sea. Born on the misty heights of Plynlimon, the Severn (or Hafren) seeps sluggishly and inauspiciously from a squelching sphagnum bog, but in no time at all it is gathering strength and well into its torrent stage, enlivened by falls and cascades as it plunges headlong through Hafren Forest. At this stage its acid, well-oxygenated but mineral-poor water supports an abundance of insects and a few fish such as trout, although the flow is too fast for plants to establish a hold.

Surprisingly quickly, the steep, V-shaped valley is left behind as tributaries join the main stream, which widens and slows as it descends into the agricultural valleys of Mid Wales. The water, warmer now and increasingly nutrient-rich, already supports a fine array of plants and an increasing number of coarse fish, as well as salmon and trout. By the time it enters Shropshire, the Severn has matured into a crazily meandering river cut deeply into its floodplain, its steep banks lined with willows and alders. At Buildwas it changes character again, surging through Ironbridge Gorge before turning south through a delectable, well-wooded landscape to Bridgnorth, and then on to Bewdley, Stourport and Worcester. Below Worcester the river is broader and slower, but its erosive power has not been lost altogether, as cliffs such as Wainlode demonstrate.

South of Gloucester, the Severn is tidal and the huge, sweeping Arlingham Loop leads to The Noose and Frampton Sand, the first real precursors of the estuary to come. Soon the Severn Sea, as it is known locally, is redolent with an unmistakable maritime flavour as the scent of seaweed brings a hint of the distant Atlantic to the lush watermeadows of the river's hinterland.

On its final approach to the sea the Severn is carrying immense quantities of material eroded from its upper reaches, most of which goes to reinforce the mudflats and sandbanks built up over millennia and now providing rich feeding grounds for countless thousands of waders and wildfowl. Bleak but exhilarating, this windswept estuary is at its most evocative in winter, when skeins of geese slice through the huge skies overhead.

The Source of the River Severn

The Severn has the second highest tidal range in the world, as well as the celebrated tidal wave known as the Severn Bore, formed by the incoming tide rushing upstream and being funnelled along an ever-narrowing channel so that the water is forced up in a great wave. The best places to watch the bore are Minsterworth, Elmore, Stonebench, Longney and Epney. The largest bores are created by high tides, which occur in each lunar cycle, but especially in spring and autumn.

The Severn's significance to man was originally strategic. It served as a highway and a barrier, a link with the outside world and a defence against marauders. It was also a rich source of food, harbouring practically every species of British freshwater fish, including twaite shad, whose breeding strongholds are on the Severn and the Wye. As early as 1285, an Act specified a close season for salmon, which were traditionally caught in nets or in open-mouthed, conical baskets known as putcheons, or putchers, mounted in racks on the mudbanks. The salmon catch has declined steadily this century and there are strict laws to protect dwindling stocks.

Below Tewkesbury the elver catch is big business in spring. Elvers are young eels that hatch in the Sargasso Sea and are carried eastwards by the Gulf Stream. They enter the Severn in millions and are hand-netted by licensed elvermen wherever the current carries them close to the bank. Historically they were a popular delicacy on Severnside, but are now an unaffordable luxury and are exported live from Sharpness to stock foreign fish farms.

The river's principal role in the past was a commercial one, with all manner of goods carried, including exotic foreign imports brought upstream from Bristol. Though the main ports were Bridgnorth, Bewdley, Worcester and Gloucester, there were also many quays serving small towns, villages and hamlets. By the end of the 17th century the Severn was busier than any other European river except the Meuse. Less than 100 years later trade was further boosted when the canal system linked the Severn with the industrial Midlands.

For centuries, the punt was the commonest boat on the Severn, used for fishing, ferrying and general carrying. Coracles were in common use too, persisting until 1939 between Shrewsbury and Arley. Larger vessels, however, were needed for trading and, by the mid-15th century, the most common trading vessel was flat-bottomed with a square sail. Over the next 200 years it evolved into the Severn trow, which came in large and small versions. The larger ones operated on the estuary and in the Bristol Channel as well as on the lower reaches of the Severn, while smaller ones worked the shallow upper river. Special small trows were also built to carry salt from Droitwich down to Gloucester after the opening of the Droitwich Canal in 1771. With the introduction of steam tugs in the 1840s, most trows were derigged to become towed barges and a few remained in service well into the 20th century.

The Severn was originally tidal up to Worcester, and navigable almost as far as Welshpool, but the navigation was never an easy one. Water levels were very low in summer and above Gloucester the river was little more than a series of pools separated by rock bars with minimal depth of water above them. Trows would proceed downstream using a combination of sailpower and the river's flow, but journeys upstream were accomplished by teams of bow-hauliers harnessed to a towing rope. It was hard work, but they were hard men

and strongly resisted the introduction of horses, though by 1812 a horse towpath stretched from Shrewsbury to Gloucester.

As boats increased in size so did navigational problems. By the end of the 18th century, Bewdley was becoming the natural upper limit, while the shifting shoals and sandbanks south of Gloucester were seriously affecting trade. Substantial improvements were necessary and in 1793 an Act authorised the building of a canal from Gloucester to Berkeley Pill. Work immediately began on Gloucester Docks, but it was 1827 before the canal was completed and then only to Sharpness. Nevertheless, it gave a tremendous boost to trade and in 1842 the Severn Commission was formed to improve the navigation of the upper Severn. Locks and weirs were built, causing the upper tidal limit to move south to Gloucester. The river was dredged and a minimum depth maintained thereafter.

Fly agaric; beautiful, yet poisonous

Stourport Canal Basin

In 1890, further improvements were made to encourage larger vessels from the channel ports, but the river was losing out to the railway, and the 20th-century growth of road transport dealt another blow. However, in the 1920s petroleum became an important commodity and the Severn's temporary salvation. It was carried by narrowboats and dumb barges, towed by steam tugs, until 1935 when a fleet of sea-going motor tanker barges was introduced. The peak years for petrol and oil traffic, with the barges operating from Swansea to Stourport, were from 1942 to 1955, ending in 1967 when a network of pipelines was opened. Today the only commercial traffic, apart from pleasure steamers, is a pair of motor barges that carry grain from Sharpness to Healing's Flour Mill at Tewkesbury.

However, the river is still of great value. It provides water for agricultural, industrial and domestic users and is the centre of a growing tourist and leisure industry.

Efforts must be made to ensure that all this isn't to the detriment of its other main role as a vital habitat for wildlife. Much of the Severn's catchment area is agricultural so it is relatively free of industrial pollutants, but agricultural pollution is a problem in places. Despite this, it has considerable wildlife value. In recent years it has been recolonised by otters, whose numbers are now increasing after falling to dangerously low levels. Below Frampton the tidal estuary is of international importance for birds, with vast mudflats for wintering and passage waders, especially dunlin, which peak at over 50,000 on the estuary as a whole. The riverside grazing meadows near Slimbridge are the winter home of one of the main flocks of white-fronted geese in southern Britain, while large numbers of shelduck sit out their annual moult (when they are rendered temporarily flightless) in Bridgwater Bay.

The following codes of good practice are intended to be understood and used by all walkers, but in the context of the Severn Way long-distance route, are primarily aimed at day or casual walkers.

SAFE WALKING CODE

- During or following prolonged wet weather, check the river level by telephoning:
ENVIRONMENT AGENCY CUSTOMER SERVICES 01743 272828
- Take care during or following wet weather when paths can become slippery
- Always wear suitable clothing and footwear; paths can be muddy and many paths are bordered by overhanging vegetation, which can damage clothing or scratch or sting bare flesh
- Carry spare and waterproof clothing, refreshments, a small first aid kit, the relevant map, a torch and a whistle, in case you get into difficulty
- Plan your walk with care, especially if you are walking alone, and make sure someone knows where you are going and when you expect to be back
- If you are using public transport be sure to check timetables

COUNTRYSIDE COURTESY

- Use public transport wherever possible in preference to a car or motorcycle
- If you do use a car, avoid parking it in a way that causes obstruction or damage. Avoid roadside verges, gateways and passing places
- Keep to rights of way or clearly marked areas of public access when crossing farmland
- Use only gates or stiles to cross field boundaries
- Close all gates that you have opened
- Avoid disturbing wildlife, including plants and trees
- Keep dogs under close control and always clean up after them
- Guard against all risk of fire
- Make no unnecessary noise
- Take your litter home, or dispose of it safely
- Support local businesses and services wherever possible
- Enjoy the countryside and respect the ways of life and work you encounter

EASY ACCESS

The Severn Way Partnership aspires to make the route accessible to as many people as possible. However, accessibility varies along the route and according to weather and river conditions. For details of the route's suitability for your needs telephone the Countryside or Rights of Way Section at the relevant local authority for the part of the route that you are intending to use - details on page 102

DISCLAIMER The route of the Severn Way is subject to constant upgrading and improvement. At times the route may vary from the published map and text. Any variations in the route will be shown, at the appropriate point, by waymarkers and map boards advising walkers of the revised route. Although every effort has been made to ensure the accuracy of the information contained in this publication, neither the publishers nor the agents can accept responsibility for any errors or omissions, nor for any actions taken, or not taken, as a result of the information presented.

The following notes are intended for walkers undertaking the Severn Way in its entirety or in multi-day sections.

Day or casual walkers will find the notes useful, but should also refer to the section on Countryside Codes, which relate to walkers undertaking short duration routes.

PREPARATION AND FITNESS

Fit, healthy and experienced walkers accustomed to long days of walking will encounter no difficulty in tackling the Severn Way, but it would be foolish even to think about setting off if you have not previously done any extended walking or had to carry a heavy pack. Getting yourself into condition is neither an arduous nor an unpleasant process, and every walk you do in preparation will make your experience and enjoyment of the Way all the better.

Nor does conditioning extend only to you. It is vitally important, for example, that you avoid wearing new boots that are not broken in, or clothing that has not had the chance to lose its newness. Comfort on a long walk can be critically important; discomfort can be painful if allowed to go on too long. If you do feel blisters coming on, or your boots start rubbing around the ankles, do attend to the problem sooner rather than later.

WHEN TO DO IT

Many people, perhaps because of family or work commitments and obligations, may have little freedom over when they choose to tackle a long walk. But, if possible, there are certain times to be avoided, sometimes for less obvious reasons than the congestion you can expect during the main tourist months of July and August. Certainly, if you can avoid these months, you are less likely to find accommodation fully booked. This is especially important on the Severn Way, where accommodation is limited in places. In any event, it is always wise to plan your route carefully and to book accommodation well ahead.

WAYMARKING

The Severn Way is waymarked throughout its length. However, work to standardise this is on-going and waymarks are susceptible to floods and vandalism.

MAPS

The maps in this guide are diagrammatic, and will not guide you across complex field and farm layouts (mainly in Powys). For this reason, you should consider taking Ordnance Survey maps. But until the OS completes development of its Explorer Series of maps covering the route of the Severn Way (probably during 1999), walkers will find they need the following Pathfinder, Explorer and Outdoor Leisure maps, or the Landrangers. These are:

Pathfinders
928: Llanidloes
929: Llandinam and Dolfor
908: Newtown
887: Llanfair Caereinion
888: Welshpool
868: Middletown and Nesscliffe
869: Shrewsbury
889: Dorrington and Cressage
890: Ironbridge and Telford (South)
911: Bridgnorth and Much Wenlock
932: Highley
952: Wyre Forest and Cleobury Mortimer
953: Kidderminster and Bromsgrave
974: Droitwich
996: Worcester

Explorers
14*: Malvern Hills
154: Bristol West
167: Thornbury, Dursley and Yate
* the number of this map will change to 190 with new editions of Explorers.

Outdoor Leisure Map
14: Wye Valley and Forest of Dean

or the following Landrangers
136, 126, 127, 138, 150, 162, 172

DAILY ITINERARIES

You must plan your daily walk according to your own strengths and abilities. The basic walk is 337km (210 miles) in length, which, ideally, gives 14 days of 24km (15 miles) walking. Most people would find this comfortable, but it makes no allowance for rest days, nor the fact that the route does not always fit conveniently into this pattern.

The Severn Way, however, is not a forced march, something you have to do in so many days (unless, of course, commitments mean that you do). The Way is a walk to be enjoyed at leisure; something to take your time over and to use as a gateway to exploration of the countryside that lies to either side of it.

EQUIPMENT

All walkers have their own preferences in the matter of equipment and clothing. When extending day walking into multiple day walking much the same general items are needed, with the emphasis on being able to stay warm and dry (as much as possible), and comfortable in all weather conditions.

The following list may be found a useful reminder - rucksack (comfortable, well padded, appropriate to backpacking rather than day walking, and preferably already used by you, if only on trial walks), boots, socks (and spare socks), trousers (or shorts, etc., but not shorts alone - at certain times of the year there are a lot of nettles), underclothes, shirt, midwear (e.g. pullover) and spare, wind/waterproof jacket and overtrousers, hat, gloves, maps, compass, torch (with spare battery and bulbs), whistle, first aid kit, survival bag or space blanket, food and drink, insect repellent, ablution tackle, including half a roll of toilet tissue (for emergencies), small hand towel.

Campers will also need such additional weighty items as tent, sleeping bag, karrimat, cooking equipment and utensils.

Pedal bin liners will be found to have a number of useful purposes: keeping wet clothes separate from dry in the sack, containing burst packets of food, cereal, etc., and rubbish, until a suitable disposal point can be reached, and for insulating dry socks from wet boots when walking.

With limited opportunities along the Way to obtain cash, it becomes vitally important that you estimate your money requirements in advance. There are banks in all the main centres, and a chequebook and banker's card can generally be used to obtain cash from post offices, which are found in many villages. The best advice is that if you need cash, be sure to get it in the main towns.

WALES
Powys

ENGLAND
Shropshire

Welshpool

Shrewsbury

● Ironbridge

Telford

PLYNLIMON

Bridgnorth

Newtown

● Caersws

● Llanidloes

Worcestershire

Bewdley ●

Stourport-on-Severn

N

Worcester

Upton upon Severn ●

Gloucestershire
Tewkesbury

Gloucester

South
Gloucestershire

BRISTOL
CHANNEL

BRISTOL
LINK

Bristol
Bristol

KEY TO MAPS

- City or large town ● Town
- **Motorway**
- Road
- *River*/Canal
- Forest/Woods
- Route of the Severn Way walk
- Field boundaries
- ❶ Places of interest, detailed in text
- 🚆 Railway station
- Severn Valley Railway
- Severn Valley Railway Station
- Picnic Site
- Country Park
- Nature Reserve
- Golf Course
- P Public Car Park
- Public Telephone
- PH Public House
- + Church/Abbey

THE LONGEST RIVERSIDE WALK IN BRITAIN
337KM - 210 MILES
FROM SOURCE TO SEA

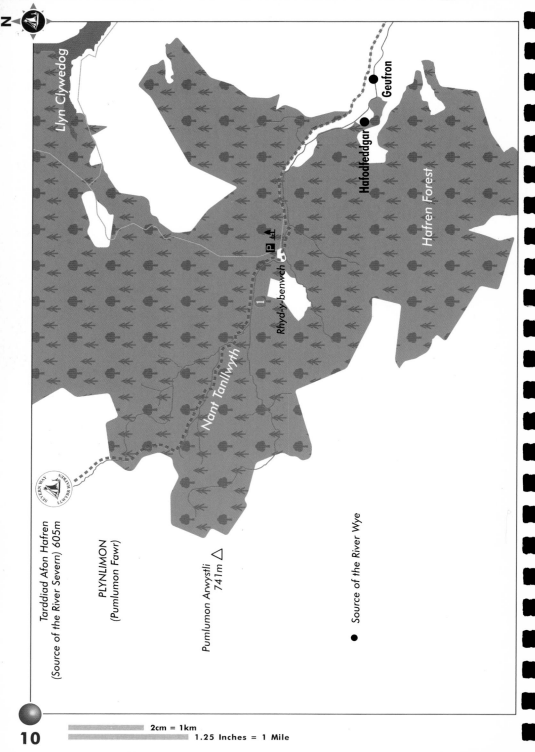

N

Llyn Clywedog

Geufron

Hafodfeddgar

Hafren Forest

Rhyd-y-benwch

P

Nant Tanllwyth

SEVERN WAY
HAFREN

Tarddiad Afon Hafren
(Source of the River Severn) 605m

PLYNLIMON
(Pumlumon Fawr)

Pumlumon Arwystli
741m △

● Source of the River Wye

2cm = 1km
1.25 Inches = 1 Mile

PLYNLIMON

Black's 'Picturesque Guide to North Wales' describes Plynlimon as 'the most dangerous mountain in Wales', owing to the 'frequency of bogs, concealed under a smooth and apparently firm turf'. He, and others that followed him, with the exception of the redoubtable George Borrow, who strode across the mountain on his journey through 'Wild Wales', displayed a timidity characteristic of the times. Coupled with the fearsome uncertainty of what lay in this remote region is the fact that Plynlimon has also featured in Welsh history as a place of turmoil and bloodshed. Its morasses, few in reality, have witnessed many a struggle. It was on the slopes of Plynlimon in 1401 that the ubiquitous Owain Glyndŵr gave renewed impetus to his rebellion against the English with an important military victory, before going on to sack Montgomery, burn Welshpool and destroy the Abbey of Cwmhir.

But the greatest feature of Plynlimon is surely a geographical one, for the mountain's peaty folds give rise to several watercourses, including two major rivers, the Wye and the Severn, each exploring some of the most fertile and beautiful countryside in Wales and the Marches as they flow down to the sea. And the greatest of these, with which this guide is concerned, is the

Source of the River Severn

Severn, at 354km (221 miles) the longest river in Britain. As such, it provides an unrivalled opportunity to enjoy a fascinating source-to-sea walk.

To undertake a walk that has its starting point high in the watery wastelands of Plynlimon, however, means adding to your journey before you even begin, because of the need to first trek up to the source of the Severn in order to follow the river downstream. The nearest point to the source which is accessible by road is the picnic area and car park at Rhyd-y-benwch in Hafren Forest. Taxis from Llanidloes are inexpensive, and provide the fastest way of reaching the picnic area, though a Royal Mail post bus also operates.

Rhyd-y-benwch stands on the site of a farmhouse, though only a meadow and a few old ash trees give any clue to this today. All around are conifers, just some of the millions of trees which make up the Forestry Commission's huge Hafren Forest, planted since the

1920's. Today, as they are felled, many of the conifers are being replaced by native species, thus creating a mosaic of habitats for wildlife.

GETTING THERE

From Rhyd-y-benwch turn down a path that leads instantly to the Severn, a more slender version of what will be encountered later in the journey. Pass a ford and go forward onto a boardwalk, which can be very slippery after rain. The attractive waterfall at the end of the boardwalk was used by generations of shepherds for washing their sheep, and is worthy of attention before continuing on a waymarked route (blue-and white-banded posts) through trees and on past a flume station to meet a broad stony track. At its confluence with the Afon Hore the Severn changes direction, with a path skirting trees to the first bridge-crossing of the river.

Shortly after the bridge the upward route leaves the Severn to pass the instruments of a meteorological station and to follow a course alongside the Nant Tanllwyth, climbing steeply to a forest road. Cross the road and continue climbing, now with only white-topped posts and the Tanllwyth as guides. Cross another forest road, turning briefly left then right, and climb still higher until the path emerges onto the top forest road, opposite a ride covered with heather and bilberry. Turn right and follow a descending track until you meet the Severn once more, at this stage just a mountain stream. Leave the track here and walk through a plantation alongside the Severn before emerging, at a stile, onto the bleak open hillside of Plynlimon.

The highest point of this upland expanse (Pen Pumlumon Fawr, 752m/2,467ft) is still some distance away, but the source of the Severn is much closer, and you are guided to it by an intermittent line of white-topped posts. Only near the very source is the going less than straightforward and even here the worst of the peaty hollows can be avoided by simple circumnavigation. The official source, a small reedy pool, is marked by two large posts.

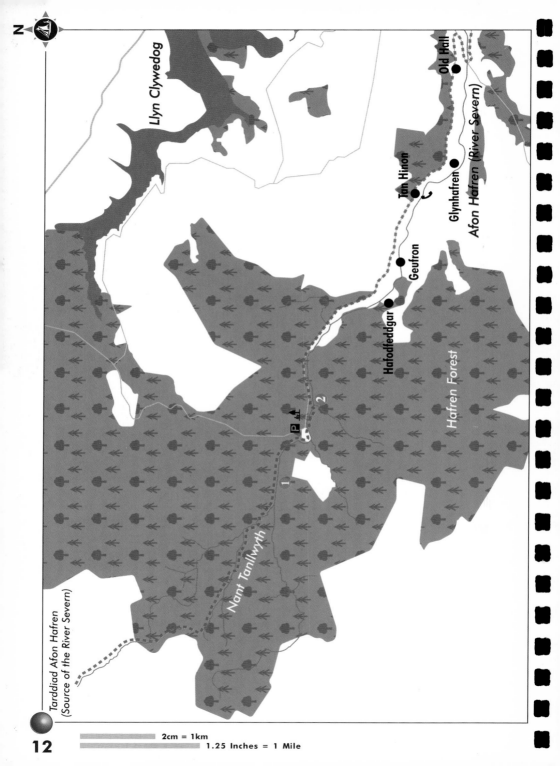

N

Llyn Clywedog

Old Hall

Tan Hinon

Glynhafren

Afon Hafren (River Severn)

Geufron

Hafodfeddigar

Hafren Forest

P 🚻 ⛺

2

1

Nant Tanllwyth

Tarddiad Afon Hafren
(Source of the River Severn)

2cm = 1km
1.25 Inches = 1 Mile

INTO HAFREN FOREST

Leave the source of the River Severn, above which red kite and peregrine frequently patrol, by heading back towards Hafren Forest, following a line of white-topped posts through a brief expanse of blanket bog. Soon, on the north-eastern side of the infant Severn, you are on a grassy path which descends to a stile at the upper boundary of Hafren Forest. The path goes into the trees, continuing for a short distance to a wide forest trail. Turn right here, crossing the Severn for the first time. Already it is an ebullient stream muscling its way through plantations of pine and spruce.

When, a little over 1km (half a mile) later, you reach an open ride on the right, covered with heather and bilberry, branch left at a waymark, going down through a narrow forest break to a footbridge. After this you re-enter plantation, where the path descends beside a stream and shortly meets another broad trail. Turn left for about 40m/yds, and then leave the trail, turning right, back into plantation. Descend beside the Nant Tanllwyth to another broad trail on the edge of a clear-felled area. Go forward at this point, continuing alongside the Nant Tanllwyth, the onward route now marked by posts banded with white and blue.

In late summer and early autumn, if conditions are damp and mild, you can expect to find the trees of Hafren Forest sheltering a wide range of fungi, some of which are poisonous. One of the most lethal of all is the deceptively attractive fly agaric, its bright red cap studded with white spots. You may also be fortunate enough to spot elusive birds such as crossbills and siskins high in the branches.

SEVERN-BREAK-ITS-NECK

As you descend beside the Nant Tanllwyth you may experience some awkwardness underfoot, caused by tree roots, which can also be slippery when wet.

Pass a flume station and cross a cleared area on a narrow footpath to rejoin the Severn just after a group of meteorological instruments. The flume is a device to measure river discharge, part of an instrument network installed to study the hydrology of the drainage basin upstream.

A footbridge takes you back onto the left bank. Shortly after the river bends to the left, at its confluence with the Afon Hore, you join a broad track. When the track forks, branch right. Stay beside the Severn to pass another flume station, and continue with the river.

A short way on, just below some small cascades ❶, you join the Hafren boardwalk, which is very slippery when wet. As you approach Rhyd-y-benwch and pass a ford, branch right on a riverside gravel path. Pass a footbridge and immediately climb left to the edge of a field. Turn right to follow the field edge, soon reaching a picnic area overlooking the river. Continue along the path, which takes you onto another slippery boardwalk and then into forest. After leaving the trees, cross a bridge to the right bank, and follow a broad track until you reach a bridge at the waterfall known as Severn-Break-its-Neck ❷.

Cross the bridge and go up the bank, turning right to reach the valley road. As you emerge from the forest so the valley opens up in front of you, a delightful picture of rolling green hillsides, patterned by hedgerows, that accompanies you down the road to Neuadd (Old Hall).

Whenever the route closely follows the river, keep an eye open, too, for dippers and grey wagtails, which are perfectly suited to this watery habitat.

Severn-Break-its-Neck Falls

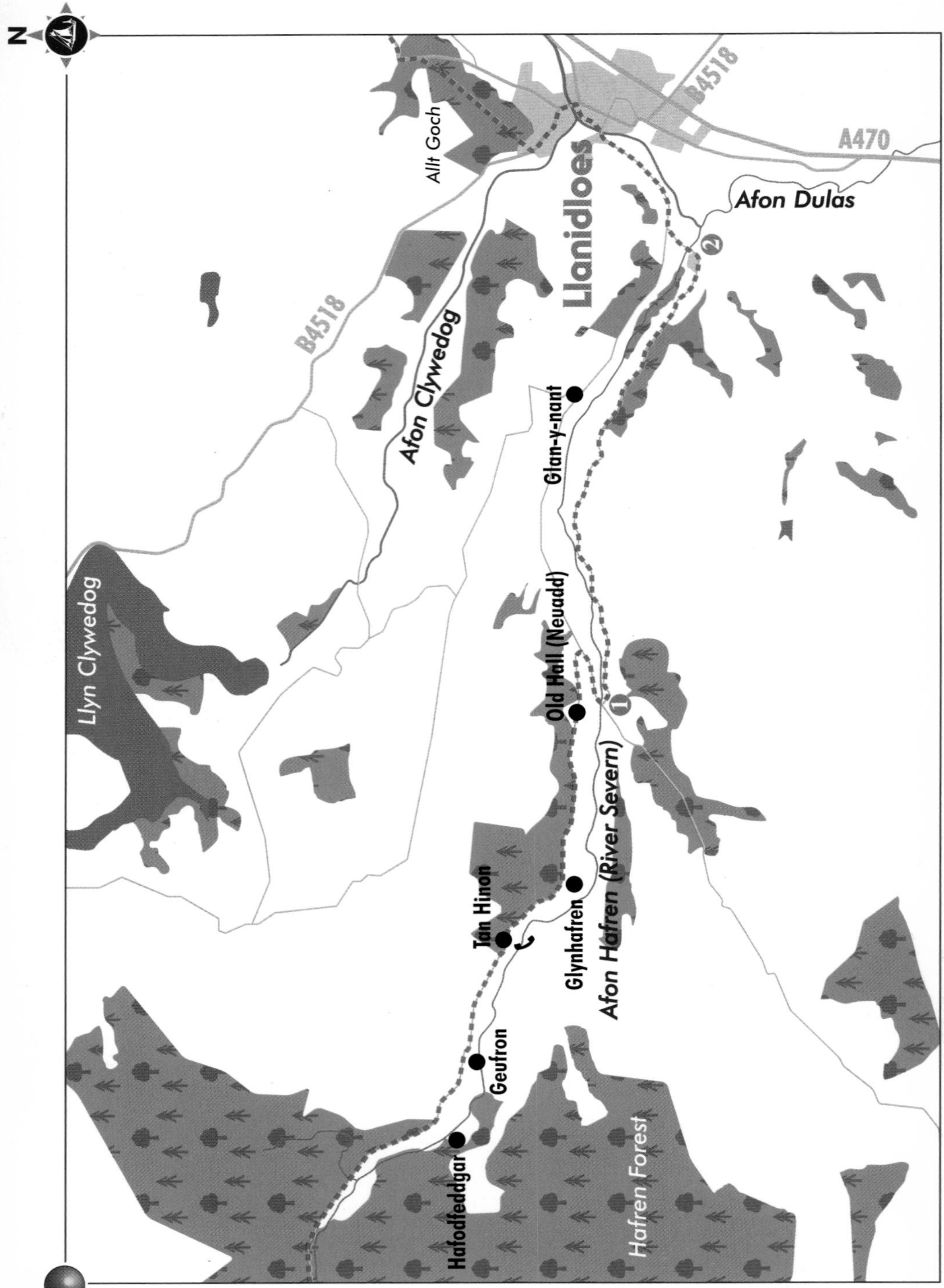

N

B4518

A470

Allt Goch

Llanidloes

Afon Dulas

②

B4518

Afon Clywedog

Glan-y-nant

Llyn Clywedog

Old Hall (Neuadd)

①

Afon Hafren (River Severn)

Tan Hinon

Glynhafren

Geufron

Hafren Forest

Hafodfeddgar

2cm = 1km
1.25 Inches = 1 Mile

Follow the road past Neuadd (where there is a small post office, but with limited opening hours) down to a junction. Turn right here and descend to cross the Severn, then immediately turn left on a lane. Pass the Old Chapel ❶ at Glanhafren. After a cattle grid, keep left, following a quiet back lane for almost 4km (2½ miles) to a T-junction. Turn left and cross the Severn again at Felindre Bridge ❷.

At the next road turn right and walk towards Llanidloes. Just as you reach the edge of town turn right over Short Bridge then take the first turning on the left into Penygraig Street.

LLANIDLOES

The first town on the Severn, Llanidloes is built on an area of flat land around the river's confluence with a tributary, the Clywedog. The Dulas also joins the Severn nearby, at the south end of Llanidloes, but the original town, including the church, developed by the confluence with the Clywedog, near a ford where ancient trackways converged. The little settlement received a considerable boost to its fortunes in 1280, when Edward I granted a market charter, and the street plan which subsequently developed still survives to some extent. The buildings that line the streets of Llanidloes today are a beguiling mix of periods and styles, with the emphasis on Georgian and Victorian, enlivened by a few half-timbered structures from earlier centuries. Most distinguished of these is the market hall, a timber-framed building of c1600 which stands in the centre of town and is the only one of its kind surviving in Wales. The arcaded lower part is open to the street and was originally filled with market stalls. Stout wooden pillars support an upper storey which has had a variety of uses in the past and now houses a museum.

The church of St Idloes stands on a riverside site said to have been chosen by the saint himself in the 7th century. The present building, however, dates only from the 14th century, though it does contain some earlier work - a fine arcade of c1195-1220, which is believed to have been salvaged from the Abbey of Cwmhir at the time of the Dissolution of the Monasteries. The same may be true of the lovely hammerbeam roof with its winged angels. Outside, the most obvious feature is the massive 14th-century west tower topped with a two-stage timber belfry typical of Montgomeryshire. The church was substantially rebuilt in the 1540s and restored in 1880-82.

Llanidloes was once important as a centre for lead-mining, wool-producing and weaving. It was badly hit by the depression of the early 19th century and in 1839 became involved in the Chartist movement, which sought to improve the lot of ordinary workers through electoral reform. The government, afraid of revolution, was extremely nervous of any dissent. Llanidloes weavers were particularly, and justifiably, discontented with their working conditions and wages. Agitators stirred up feeling and when a few men were found with guns they were imprisoned, despite claims they were only after rabbits. Fighting broke out and over-reaction by the authorities led to riots, with some local men subsequently transported to Australia for their part in the troubles. Today, peaceful again, Llanidloes still functions as a market town serving the surrounding countryside.

Great Oak Street is the most attractive thoroughfare in town, and where you will find many of the shops, pubs, restaurants and cafés which offer a warm welcome to residents and visitors alike.

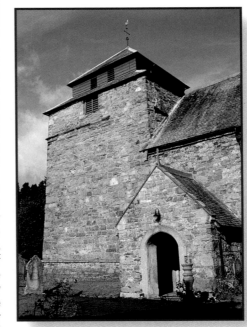

Church of St Idloes, Llanidloes

Top: Bridge and statue in Llandinam. Bottom: Market Hall in Llanidloes.

LLANIDLOES is the first town on the Severn, and a place of considerable interest. Historically, its roots go deep, the settlement having developed at a point where prehistoric trackways converged on a fording point of the river. Llanidloes became an important centre for lead-mining, wool-producing and flannel-weaving but was hard hit by the depression of the early 19th century. Today, it is increasingly appreciated as a good centre from which to explore the surrounding area, for it occupies that transitional zone where the bleak moors of Plynlimon sweep down to meet the lush valleys, combining the virtues of two very different types of landscape. The Plynlimon range is often dismissed as featureless moorland but it has its own wild beauty: a mosaic of grass, heather and sphagnum, it is enlivened by water in all its forms. It squelches underfoot and it pours from the sky, but it also feeds numerous pools, streams and waterfalls, and no less than five major rivers have their origin here: Severn, Wye, Rheidol, Ystwyth and Clywedog.

The wildlife of the upper Severn has had to adapt to what is now largely a man-made landscape, ranging from the conifers of Hafren Forest to the intensively farmed floodplain near the border with England. However, birds such as crossbill, siskin, goshawk and long-eared owl certainly find Hafren Forest much to their liking, and the actual source of the Severn lies in red kite country, giving the walker a good chance of seeing one of these magnificent raptors. Buzzards are far more common, and are themselves majestic birds, but look carefully at every "buzzard" - if it has a forked tail it's a kite. If the light is good and you have binoculars you should be able to make out the beautiful colouring which further distinguishes the red kite from other raptors. Not so long ago red kites were perched on the very brink of extinction in Britain, with only a tiny population hanging on in Mid Wales. Since then, efforts to save them have proved so successful that kites have now been reintroduced to England and Scotland, but Mid Wales remains their heartland.

On the Severn itself, the endearing dipper and the exquisite kingfisher are frequently seen, while autumn brings an influx of whooper swans to feed in the riverside meadows of Penstrowed, between Caersws and Newtown. The elusive otter is thriving once again throughout the upper Severn catchment but you would be very fortunate to see one. Nor are you likely to glimpse the nocturnal badger, another mammal which is flourishing here, but rabbit, squirrel and fox are often seen. Look out for the water vole (Ratty of "Wind in the Willows" fame) which is increasingly rare but still occurs on the Severn.

At Llanidloes the Severn is joined by the Afon Clywedog, which, a few miles upstream, has been dammed to form a reservoir, Llyn Clywedog. This provides some water locally and a small amount of electricity is also generated, but it was built primarily to regulate the flow of the Severn. During dry weather the natural flow of the river is augmented by the release of water from Llyn Clywedog, and in the winter excess water is allowed to build up in the reservoir to avoid flooding. All the same, heavy rain in the upper and middle catchments can cause such a rapid rise that flooding is often inevitable, as riverside residents downstream know only too well. In terms of landscape use, the construction of the reservoir represents the biggest change ever to occur in what was once the most spectacular of the valleys cut into the Plynlimon range. The water has its own attraction, however, and the combination of glorious scenery with recreational facilities (fishing and sailing) makes Llyn Clywedog popular with visitors. There is a variety of wildlife habitats here, and birdwatchers should find it rewarding, with buzzards and ravens patrolling the skies, redpolls and willow warblers feeding in the trees, common sandpipers on the shore and cormorants and goosanders on the lake itself.

Downstream of Llanidloes, but across the river from the Severn Way, and unseen by walkers, lies Llandinam, the birthplace in 1818 of the industrialist and Liberal MP, David Davies, who built Barry Docks to facilitate the export of iron and coal from South Wales. He was also heavily involved with building the railway system of Mid Wales. A memorial statue to him stands in the village.

Llandinam is, however, now more famous for the largest wind farm in Europe. The massive turbines stride for several miles across the hills which rise to the east and south of the Severn, and some of them are visible from the Severn Way. A source of clean, green power or an unwarranted blot on the landscape? The jury is still out on that one.

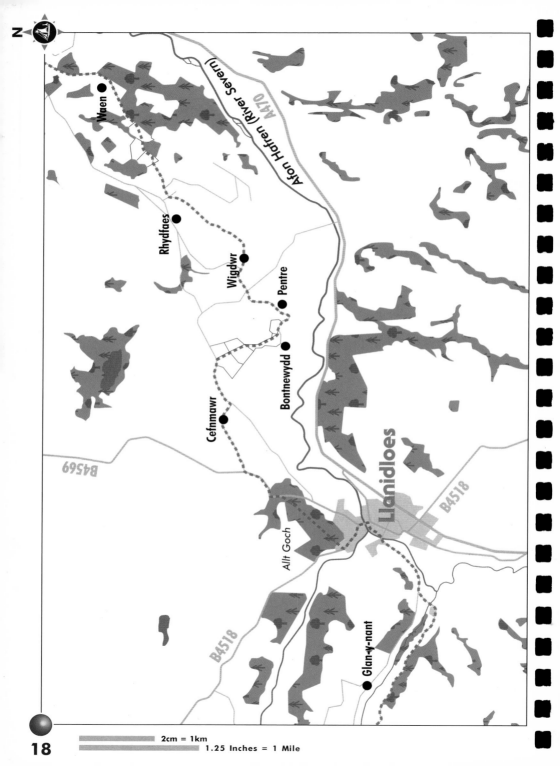

N

Waen

Afon Hafren (River Severn)

A470

Rhydfaes

Wigdwr

Pentre

Bontnewydd

Cefnmawr

B4569

Llanidloes

B4518

Allt Goch

B4518

Glan-y-nant

2cm = 1km
1.25 Inches = 1 Mile

Leave Llanidloes along Penygraig Street. As you approach the church, go left on a path down to the riverside, and follow this past the confluence with the Clywedog. Turn left over Long Bridge and then left into Westgate Street. Go uphill until, after the second turning into Tan yr Allt, you can leave the road by turning right onto a footpath climbing into wooded Allt Goch.

ALLT GOCH

The land at Allt Goch and Pen yr Allt was unenclosed common until 1816, when, under the terms of the Enclosure Act, it was divided among various landowners. Much of it is wooded, and now owned by Llanidloes Town Council, which acquired it in 1936. Parts were replanted in the early 1990s, with native broad-leaved trees replacing alien conifers.

The on-going path climbs steeply through the wood before descending to the Trefeglwys road, where you turn left. As the road bends to the right and you climb above the woodland, an inviting view of the Severn valley opens up ahead.

At the highest point of the road, turn right onto a hedged green lane. When you enter a large open pasture keep along the right-hand boundary to rejoin the continuation of the lane, and go forward between hedges.

At Cefnmawr Farm turn right, pass the farm and follow its access to a road. Turn left. When the road forks, stay right. When it starts to go downhill, turn right onto a broad descending track. At the bottom go through the right-hand one of two gates and forward, with a fence on your left, to another gate. Beyond, turn right, now going ahead with a fence and hedge on your left.

Descend through gorse and bracken to a gate, with Bontnewydd Farm below you on the right. Continue across the top edge of a sloping pasture to a farm access and cattle grid. Follow the access down and around a horseshoe bend and then climb to pass Pentre Farm.

Cross a road when you reach it, going forward to Wigdwr Farm, where the lane bends left. At the bend, go ahead through a gate onto a rising track that fashions a delightful route across sloping hill pastures. This is not only beautiful countryside but also a perfect habitat for buzzard and raven alike. Beyond a single gate the track ceases and a path now crosses the edge of a small enclosure with a brook at the bottom. On the far

side join a holloway and go through another gate, beyond which the holloway rises to a lane.

Turn left, then immediately right onto another lane. When the road surfacing ends go forward onto a rough vehicle track. Follow this until it reaches the edge of woodland, then, without entering the wood, turn left along its boundary.

In the next field, continue beside the woodland boundary to a gate just beyond an access track. Go through the gate, leaving the on-going track to strike half-left across the ensuing field to the far corner, and more woodland. Turn left along its boundary to a gate in a dip. Beyond, go onto a rising grassy path, and then forward on a woodland track. Go through a gate and continue with a hedge on your left. When you emerge on a broad track, just after a metal gate, turn left.

Golden-ringed dragonfly

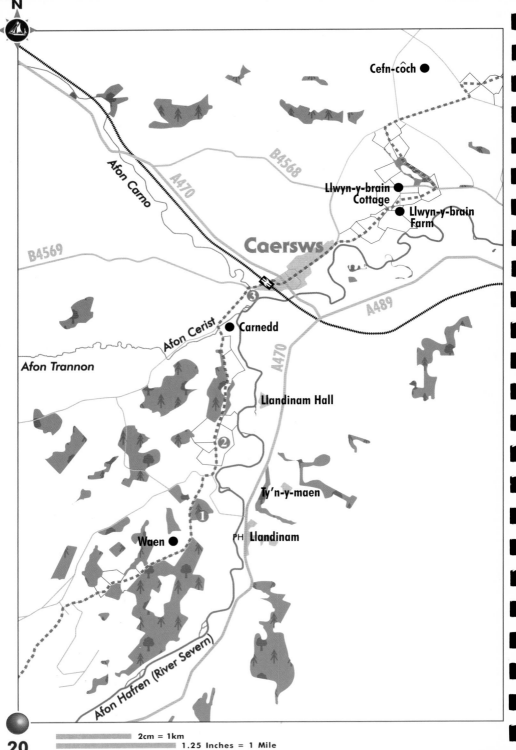

N

Cefn-côch ●

Afon Carno

A470

B4568

B4569

Llwyn-y-brain Cottage ●

Llwyn-y-brain Farm ●

Caersws

A489

Afon Cerist

● Carnedd

Afon Trannon

A470

Llandinam Hall

Ty'n-y-maen

Waen ●

PH Llandinam

Afon Hafren (River Severn)

2cm = 1km
1.25 Inches = 1 Mile

TOWARDS CAERSWS

Continue along the track, going through two gates above Waen Farm. Below you lies Llandinam, nestling in the Severn valley which rises beyond to the rolling bracken and heather heights of Moel Iart. The track then descends to pass along the left edge of Broneirion Wood ❶ to a gate. Walk down a field edge to Waen Lane and continue to a T-junction. Turn right to reach a bend, then left towards Lower Gwerneirin Farm ❷, touching briefly on the banks of the Severn for the first time since leaving Llanidloes.

At the farm keep right past buildings. Go through two gates then forward to the left of an old barn onto a rising track. When it forks, branch right onto a level green track leading to another gate. A little further on you enter a sloping field. Turn right through a double gate onto a broad grassy track along the top edge of sparse woodland. At the far side go through more gates and along a broad strip of sloping pasture, fenced on both sides. Go forward over a stile at the end of the fenced section, following a grassy track through bracken, before gradually descending to another track.

Turn left to a metal gate, beyond which a gravel track leads into a hedged path that continues past Carnedd Farm and out along a track to cross the reed-fringed Afon Cerist. Turn right along a lane to reach the B4569, where you turn right towards Caersws, immediately crossing the Afon Garno.

At the junction is a cottage ❸ where the poet John Ceiriog Hughes (1832-87) lived for a time. Hughes, a railwayman by profession, won prizes at the London, Llangollen and Merthyr Eisteddfods.

CAERSWS

It's hard to say whether Caersws is a large village or a small town, but it is certainly an important local centre for the upper Severn valley. Though unremarkable in itself, it does enjoy a lovely setting and there are some splendid walks to be had in the surrounding hills.

Caersws was an important Roman centre with a military fort, though the Romans' main interest here was probably the exploitation of Plynlimon's lead reserves. The earthworks of the fort are still discernible near the station.

Cross the railway and turn first right, following the road round into the village centre, where there are shops and pubs. Cross the A470 and go along the Aberhafesp road. Just after the last building on the left (a former hospital), as the road bends left, join a stony track on the right. Immediately go left over a stile. Turn right and head across fields towards Llwyn-y-brain Farm.

A stony track finally leads up to the farm, beside which three stiles in quick succession guide you past the buildings to a gate, from which you go half-right across a sloping pasture towards a dead tree, beyond which are another three stiles. The third one gives into a large open pasture. Cross this to another stile in the distance. One more field leads to the B4568 near Rhydlydan.

Cross the road and climb a stile to the left of a gate. Continue on a field track, soon branching left to a gate, and then go forward up a right-hand field edge. A stile at the top gives access to a large pasture. Cross this, roughly parallel with a line of oak trees, then go through a gate and on to reach a lane. Turn right to reach a junction then forward over a stile onto a hedged track that leads down to another stile. Keep on in the same direction to yet another, then go on to cross a footbridge. Continue through a strip of woodland to meet a lane near Cefn-côch Farm.

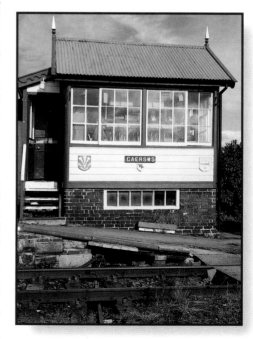

Old Cambrian Railway signal box at Caersws

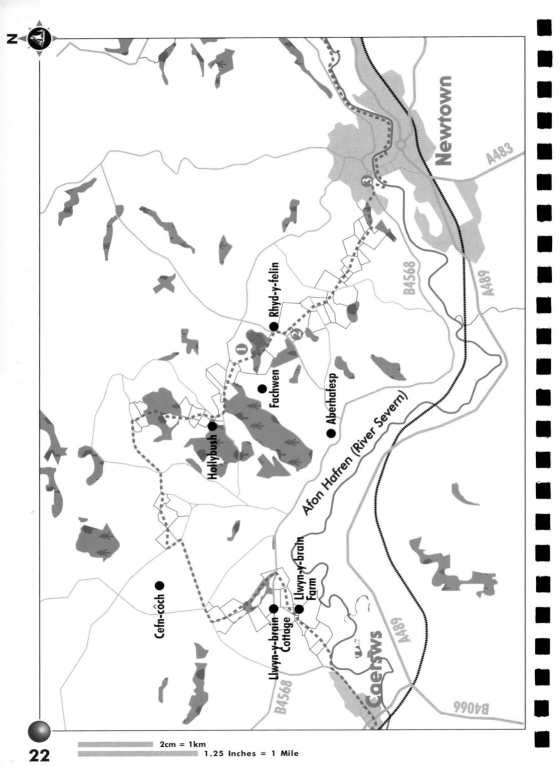

2cm = 1km
1.25 Inches = 1 Mile

HEADING FOR NEWTOWN

Turn left towards Cefn-côch Farm. After about 250m/yds leave the road on the right over a stile and go diagonally downfield to the bottom right-hand corner. Cross a footbridge and stile then turn left and continue downfield towards pylons. At the bottom, turn right alongside a fence to cross another stile and footbridge. Turn right in the ensuing field, passing below power lines to a stile beside a gate. Beyond this cross a bridge spanning a substantial stream and follow a lane to a junction, joining another lane opposite.

Keep going for 800m/yds, then turn right along a signposted vehicle track. Go through a gate, then immediately climb steeply left, alongside a hedge, before descending to cross a stream, then a stile. Go forward in the same direction across marshy ground to meet a track on the far side. Turn right and climb through woodland and up hill pasture to a track. Leave it when it bends left, going forward beside a fence to a gate at the top.

Beyond the gate, walk towards a signpost in mid-field. As you reach it, turn sharp right to climb across the shoulder of a hillside to a stile in a hedgerow. In the ensuing field, descend to the far bottom corner, and the entrance to Hollybush Farm. Turn right on a surfaced lane. When it bends right, branch left onto another lane. Shortly bear left again onto a wide track rising into woodland. Cross a stile and continue with a fence on the left, following a descending path below gorse until you reach a waymark near a large hawthorn tree. Descend towards a dip in the bottom of the field, climb a stile into a dingle, cross a footbridge and then another stile.

Cross the top edge of a field and descend to pass Fachwen Pool ❶, where water birds may sometimes be seen. After the next stile turn left to another about 150m/yds away then go forward to a lane. Turn right and go downhill. Leave the lane after about 200m/yds, turning left to Rhydfelin Baptist Chapel ❷, with its collection of beautifully inscribed slate headstones. Cross an adjacent stile and go up a tree-canopied path to an open field. Head across hill pasture towards an isolated stand of pine trees in the distance. Climb steeply until a fence deflects you up to the top corner of a field. Now a long succession of fields and waymarked stiles leads you on to reach a stile overlooking Newtown.

The town was, until comparatively recently, enclosed within a loop of the Severn but now it is spreading, though still contained within the valley by the hills you have just crossed and by the Kerry Hills to the south. In 1967 it was declared a "new town" for the second time in its history and since then the population has more than doubled.

Go downfield beside a hedge, then descend on a broad path through trees. Eventually you join a hedged path, descending to a residential street. Cross it and go forward, still descending, on a stony path which can be slippery when wet.

At the next road turn left to reach Capel Coffa, then turn right into Dolerw Park, soon passing the Gorsedd stone circle ❸, which marks the site of Newtown's Eisteddfod. Follow the path to the Severn, cross a suspension bridge and turn left on the lower of two riverside paths. After passing beneath a road bridge, to enjoy the town's facilities you can turn right up steps to the Elephant and Castle pub, then go down the main street into Newtown. The Severn Way goes under the road bridge (Long Bridge) and carries on round to cross a footbridge spanning the Severn, known locally as the Halfpenny Bridge.

Dipper

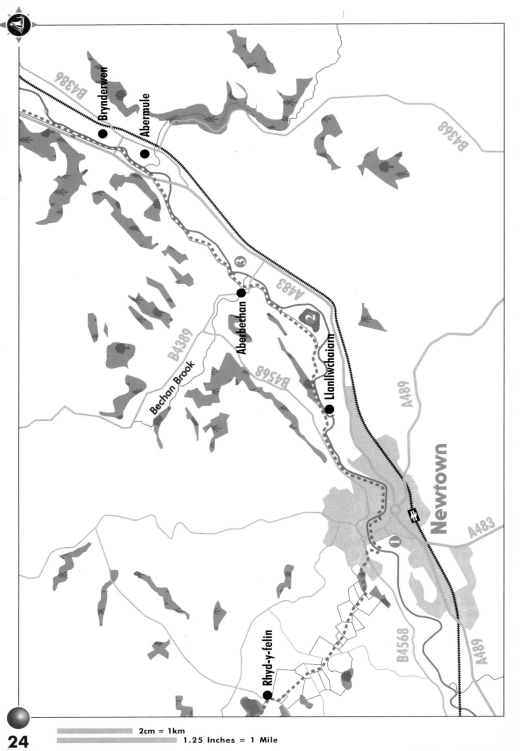

2cm = 1km

1.25 Inches = 1 Mile

NEWTOWN

Despite its name, Newtown was a market centre as long ago as the 13th century. It acquired its name in 1279 when Roger Mortimer was granted a market charter for what had previously been known as Llanfair Cedewain. The two names were used interchangeably until 1832. It is now the largest town in Mid Wales, with plenty of shops, cafés and restaurants. The Tourist Information Centre ❶ is at Back Lane, near the bus station.

The great social reformer Robert Owen, advocate of trade unions and co-operatives, was born in Newtown in 1771. There is a Memorial Museum at his birthplace, and he is buried at the tranquil riverside ruin of St Mary's Church. Don't miss the newsagent W H Smith's, occupying a splendid 1920s-style shop with a museum on the upper floor. The Textile Museum on Commercial Street is also of interest. The huge Royal Welsh Warehouse, near the station, is the home of Pryce-Jones, the world's first mail order company, patronised by Queen Victoria.

On the other side of the Severn footbridge, locally known as Halfpenny Bridge, turn right over a metal stile and walk along the floodbank. At the far end, descend to a gate and onto a path through undergrowth. Pass through the grounds of the Old Pump House, now a private residence, and onto a track that runs on to join the Montgomery Canal Walkway, constructed by Severn Trent Water in 1983, using the former canal bed and parts of the riverbank.

MONTGOMERY CANAL

Three different companies built the canal in three sections over a period of 30 years. In 1821 it finally reached Newtown, about 56km (35 miles) from its junction with the Llangollen Canal at Frankton. Limestone and coal were the main items of "up" trade (towards Newtown). The limestone, from quarries at Llanymynech, was burned in canalside kilns to provide lime for agricultural use. The main "down" trade was in timber, grain and dairy products. By 1850, the canal had become part of the network of the Shropshire Union Railway and Canal Company. It was unofficially abandoned in 1935 (officially in 1944), following a breach near Frankton, and subsequently developed into a reedy wildlife paradise. It is currently being restored to navigation, with the inevitable loss of some of its wildlife interest, though efforts are being made to minimise the damage.

The onward path past the Pwll Penarth Nature Reserve ❷ is the old towpath alongside the former canal bed, which is dry at this point. Stay on the towpath, unless you want to divert at a stile into the main part of the nature reserve. Beyond the end of the nature reserve, from Freestone Lock onwards, the canal is filled with water.

With little need for route description, the Severn Way now simply follows the towpath all the way to Welshpool. As it approaches Aberbechan the canal is carried by a triple-arched aqueduct ❸ over Bechan Brook, where the remains of a corn mill and maltings are concealed by trees.

At Abermule the route is diverted to the right to pass under a road. Continue to Brynderwen Locks where you cross to the opposite side of the canal for a short distance, before crossing back again at the next bridge, turning under it to rejoin the towpath.

Leaping salmon

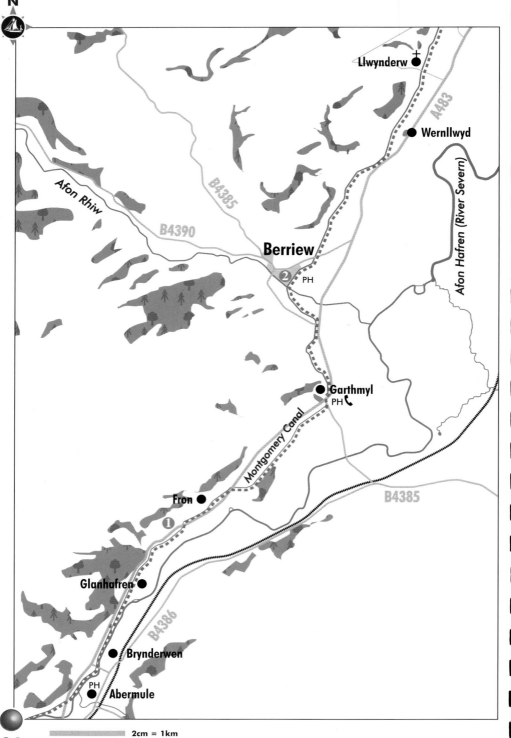

N

Llwynderw

A483

Wernllwyd

Afon Rhiw

B4385

Afon Hafren (River Severn)

B4390

Berriew

2 PH

Garthmyl
PH 📞

Montgomery Canal

Fron

1

B4385

Glanhafren

B4386

Brynderwen

PH
Abermule

2cm = 1km
1.25 Inches = 1 Mile

Brynderwen is a former coal wharf and a 19th-century warehouse still survives. Beyond Brynderwen Cottage it's towpath all the way into Welshpool; delightful, easy walking, but often too close to the A483 to enjoy the tranquillity of what is unquestionably beautiful countryside. A number of bridges add interest to this section: Glanhafren Bridge is the most ornate, with its cast iron balustrades, while Red House Bridge ❶ is one of the few remaining swing bridges on the canal. In the summer, keep an eye out for grass snakes basking in the sun, and kingfishers feeding on fish from the canal.

South of Fron the canal finally meets the busy road. Cross with care and continue on the other side. North of Fron the canal, but not the towpath, passes beneath the main road, which you have to recross to continue beside the on-going canal, finally getting a little further away from the road and the sound of traffic for a while.

On the edge of Garthmyl, where a number of wharf buildings can still be identified, you meet the B4385. Turn left to a junction, and then right on the A483. Go past the Nag's Head and branch left onto a lane which crosses the canal. Turn left to rejoin the towpath. When next you meet a road, at Refail, go forward to rejoin the towpath, and continue past the village of Berriew.

BERRIEW

The village, a pleasing arrangement of black and white cottages around a stone church, nestles below the canal embankment, but it is not a canal village as such. St Beuno founded a religious institution here in the 6th century, and a church dedicated to him was standing in the village hundreds of years before the canal was thought of. The present church is medieval but was rebuilt by the Victorians. Close by is a handsome 18th-century stone bridge spanning the River Rhiw and framed by picturesque houses, one of them flanked by some outstanding topiary.

Berriew knew great prosperity in the past as it lies in productive country at the junction of the upland sheepwalks and the lush lowland farms. The construction of the canal brought further benefits, with Berriew acting as a bridgehead of supply until the local wool trade began to suffer the effects of Australian competition.

The village's name comes from Aber-Rhiw - the place where the River Rhiw joins the Severn. A two-arched brick aqueduct carries the canal over the lovely wooded valley of the Rhiw. Originally built of stone in 1796, it has been twice rebuilt but seems sound enough now.

Anyone wanting to explore Berriew village or watch salmon leaping the waterfall in October, should leave the towpath at the aqueduct and descend to join a lane. Turn left alongside the River Rhiw and walk up towards the village. Go past the Andrew Logan Museum of Sculpture ❷ to a junction near the Talbot Inn. Turn right, crossing the Rhiw. A short way on you'll find a post office, village shops, the Lion Hotel and a telephone.

If you do visit the village, simply leave it along the B4390, until you reach the canal once more, and turn down onto the towpath. Soon you pass more locks and a garden area at a cottage. The Luggy Aqueduct, a small iron trough built in 1819, carries the canal over Luggy Brook before you pass Brithdir and Wernllwyd to reach Chapel Bridge at Llwynderw.

Black and white houses, Berriew

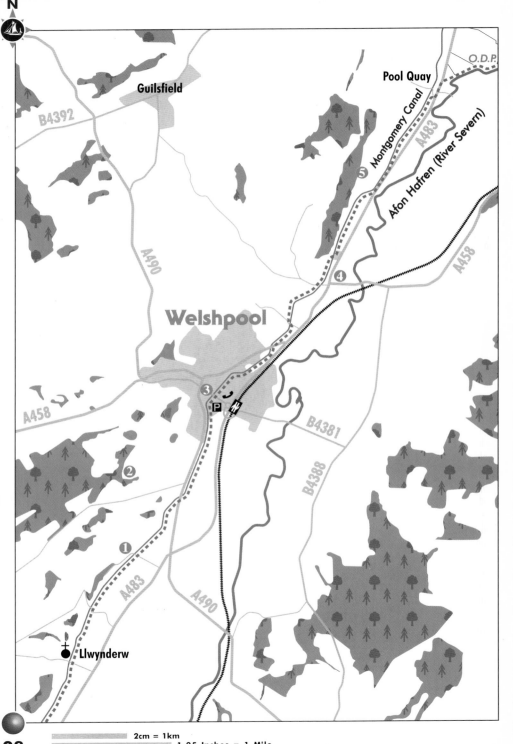

N

Guilsfield

B4392

Pool Quay

O.D.P.

Montgomery Canal

A483

Afon Hafren (River Severn)

⑤

A490

Welshpool

④

A458

A458

③

P

B4381

②

B4388

①

A483

A490

⚰ Llwynderw

2cm = 1km
1.25 Inches = 1 Mile

More easy towpath walking ensues as you continue past Llwynderw and on towards Welshpool. Before long, Belan ❶ is reached, with its recently restored locks and distinctive black and white houses, built c1800 by the canal company for the limekiln workers.

Soon after Belan, some of the parkland surrounding the National Trust's Powis Castle ❷ can be seen on the left. The castle was built in c1200 but has been much extended and embellished since. Magnificent though Powis Castle is, it is the spectacular terraced garden which is world-famous.

Not long before reaching the edge of Welshpool the canal passes beneath the main road, and continues to meet a lane. Go forward along the lane, shortly rejoining the towpath at Town Lock, and heading for the road into Welshpool, reached just after the Powysland Museum and Montgomery Canal Centre ❸.

The museum occupies a former warehouse and there are sensitively restored canal company cottages and offices nearby.

WELSHPOOL

Welshpool was granted its market charter in 1263 by Gwenwynwyn, Prince of Powys, and the town has flourished ever since. It was originally known as Pool but was renamed in 1835 to distinguish it from Poole in Dorset. The streets are lined with buildings from many periods, though it is Georgian architecture that predominates, and a thorough exploration of the town is worthwhile. The old Cambrian Railway station is superb, but now houses a shopping centre, while trains operate from a functional modern station nearby. There is also a narrow gauge line opened in 1903, the Welshpool and Llanfair Light Railway, which runs to Llanfair Caereinion from Raven Square. The Tourist Information Centre is at The Flash Leisure Centre (access from bridge 117) and Welshpool has some excellent pubs and cafés. If you arrive here on a Monday, you'll encounter Welshpool's sheep market, the largest in Europe.

Continue beneath the road bridge and along the towpath. A small aqueduct carries the canal over Lledan Brook and is followed by a girder bridge which formerly carried the Llanfair and Welshpool Railway to sidings by the Cambrian Railway station.

When you reach a road (A483), cross it and continue on the towpath to Buttington Wharf ❹. This was an important centre for the lime-burning industry that was the mainstay of the Montgomery Canal's limited commercial success, and was a place of great activity in the early 19th century.

The towpath is eventually joined by Offa's Dyke Path ❺, which shares the route of the Severn Way almost to Llandrinio. Where the two routes coincide you should follow Offa's Dyke Path.

For some time, the route has been moving ever closer to the Breidden Hills, and their bulky form will dominate much of this and the next day's walking.

When you reach Top Lock at Pool Quay the route is deflected down to the right, onto a track, and then turns right to go down to the road.

POOL QUAY

This was a Severnside settlement originally, marking the head of navigation on the river, though only in the winter was there sufficient depth of water this far upstream. The canal provided a more reliable trade route and carrying on the river had ceased by the middle of the 19th century. Pool Quay Lock on the canal is particularly attractive, and is overlooked by a pretty Victorian church with a timber belfry.

Pool Quay Lock on the Montgomery Canal

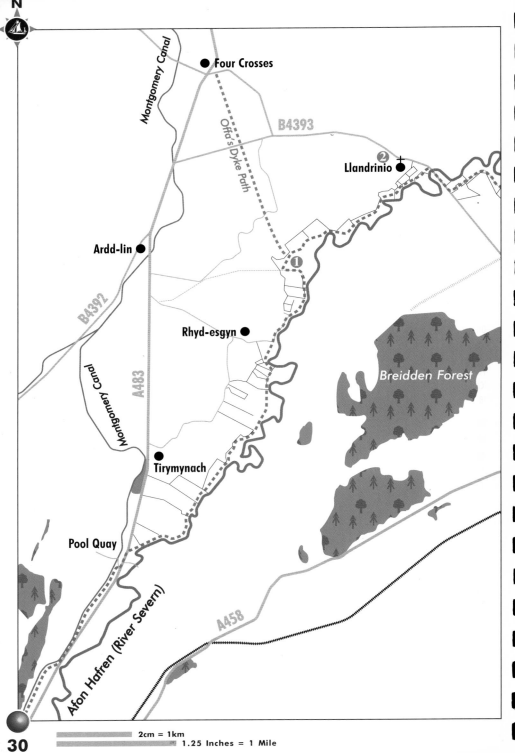

N

Montgomery Canal

● Four Crosses

B4393

Offa's Dyke Path

Llandrinio ● ❷ +

Ardd-lin ●

❶

B4392

A483

Montgomery Canal

Rhyd-esgyn ●

Breidden Forest

Tirymynach ●

Pool Quay

Afon Hafren (River Severn)

A458

2cm = 1km
1.25 Inches = 1 Mile

At the road, having now finally left the Montgomery Canal, turn left until you can rejoin Offa's Dyke Path on the opposite side of the road, immediately going left over a stile and across two fields to a footbridge. You have now rejoined the River Severn and, just after the footbridge, floodbanks may tempt you into thinking this is actually Offa's Dyke, but it isn't.

OFFA'S DYKE

Offa's Dyke Path is a long-distance footpath running through the Marches from Prestatyn in the north to Chepstow in the south. It is based upon, but doesn't always follow, the remarkable earthwork of Offa's Dyke which was built on the orders of Offa, ruler of the dominant English kingdom of Mercia from 757 to 796. The dyke is the longest archaeological monument in Britain and consists mainly of a bank, with a ditch on the Welsh side. Nobody is certain of its purpose; it may have been defensive or may merely have been intended to define the border. It is discontinuous, and it seems that in places natural features were considered sufficient - this might explain why there is no dyke along this stretch of the Severn.

Walk along the floodbank, an agreeable and easy stretch, as the route flirts with the Severn below the gaze of the shapely Breidden Hills.

BREIDDEN HILLS

These massive humps dominate the landscape for miles around. The most northerly is quarry-scarred Breidden Hill itself, topped by Rodney's Pillar, an 18th-century monument to Admiral Rodney (1719-92) who used Montgomeryshire timber for Royal Navy ships, though nationally he was more famous for defeating the French off Cape St Vincent in 1782. To the south is Moel y Golfa which also has a memorial on top, to Ernest Burton, a Romany "king" who died in 1960. There is another main summit, Middletown Hill, and a few smaller ones. Not surprisingly, there are Iron Age forts on the three main hills and a couple of lesser forts too. Sadly, in the foreground, between the Breiddens and the Severn, cluster the ugly masts of Criggion Radio Station. To the south of the Breiddens is Long Mountain, which lives up to its name.

For a while the route is deflected away from the river. It passes a sluicegate, used to manage floodwaters of the Severn, and heads along an embankment to Derwas Bridge, which spans a man-made channel, the New Cut. Cross the bridge and turn right, crossing a field to a footbridge spanning Bele Brook, a minor tributary of the Severn. Over the footbridge turn right once more, parting company with Offa's Dyke Path ❶, which shortly joins the actual dyke itself, heading roughly northwards to Llanymynech Hill, whose much-quarried slopes are visible ahead. It was these quarries that provided the limestone which was transported on the Montgomery Canal, though Llanymynech is now better known for its abundant wild flowers. Like the Breiddens and Long Mountain, Llanymynech Hill is shared between England and Wales.

Walk along the top of a grassy embankment to a stile, and then on by an obvious path towards the village of Llandrinio. Just a little to the west is Llandrinio's Norman church ❷, dedicated to St Trunio. In the porch there stands a fragment of a 10th-century stone cross.

Water avens flowers between May and September

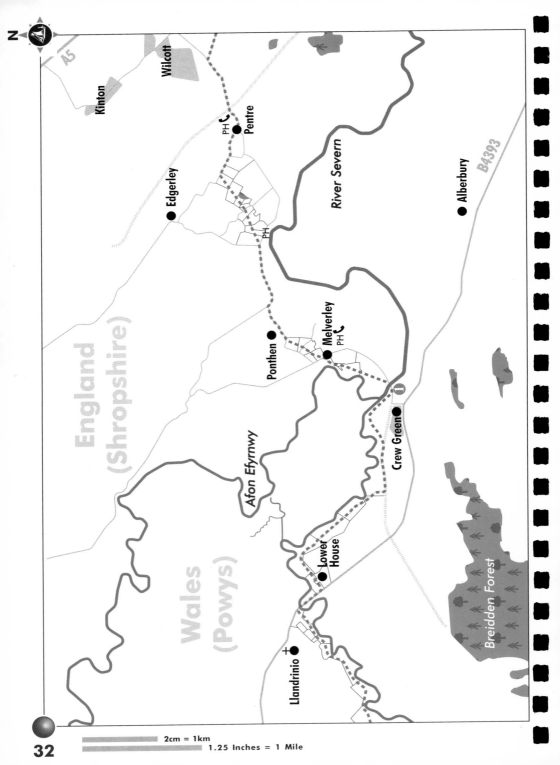

N

England (Shropshire)

Wales (Powys)

Kinton

Wilcott

A5

Pentre
PH

Edgerley

PH

River Severn

Alberbury

B4393

Melverley
PH

Ponthen

Afon Efyrnwy

Crew Green

Lower House

Breidden Forest

Llandrinio

2cm = 1km
1.25 Inches = 1 Mile

LEAVING WALES

Walk out to meet the road at Llandrinio and turn right over the bridge. After 450m/yds turn left over a stile and go along a grassy embankment to pass Lower House Farm. Briefly, the path touches on the Severn again, but then shortcuts a loop before rejoining the river at the end of a long, straight embankment.

Walk on along the embankment until you meet an obvious track heading south to the road. Go down this a short way, but, at a stile and gate, turn left. From the next stile head across a field to briefly rejoin the river, which now performs a number of serpentine loops. In the next field move away from the river, heading straight across the field, as the path shortcuts a loop. Rejoin the river and once more head across fields, passing the confluence with the Afon Efyrnwy (River Vyrnwy).

Go forward below an iron road bridge and immediately turn right to a road. Turn right again, over the bridge. As you cross the Severn here ❶, you are leaving Wales and entering the English county of Shropshire.

Immediately over the bridge branch left and cross fields towards Melverley, walking on a raised section between arable fields. When this ends, continue to the far side of the field, and follow its edge round. At farm buildings, turn right and join a road by St Peter's Church ❷, to which a visit is highly recommended.

ST PETER'S CHURCH

By late Saxon times there was already a chapel at Melverley but in 1401 this was destroyed by Owain Glyndŵr. Almost immediately, work started on a replacement, and by 1406 a new church was standing on the site. It still survives today and remains substantially unaltered except for interior embellishment and some necessary repairs. It's a very rare example of a timber, wattle and daub church. All the original beams, made from local oak, are fixed together with wooden pegs, and no nails at all were used. There is a Saxon font, which must have stood in the original church. The altar and finely carved pulpit are Jacobean.

With the Vyrnwy below its west wall, and the Severn close by, this lovely church is vulnerable to flooding and has often been cut off by the rising water, sometimes for as much as a month.

Turn right and walk to the Tontine Inn. Cross the road and a stile opposite, and head across a number of fields until you meet a road. Turn right, walking towards Pentre. The Way goes through Ponthen before branching right for Pentre. Go past Cae Howel Farm and at the next road junction go through a metal gate. (The Royal Hill Inn is a short distance further down the road.)

Cross fields to the edge of a small caravan park and go forward, continuing in the same direction, and then across a large field. Turn right for a few strides and then go left over another stile.

As the path approaches The Firs take the right-hand one of three possible footpaths to reach the road on the outskirts of Pentre. Turn right, through Pentre (telephone, Grove Inn and post office) and on along the road. Just after the entrance to Nesscliff Training Camp turn right for Wilcott Marsh and Shrawardine.

River Severn from Crew Green Bridge

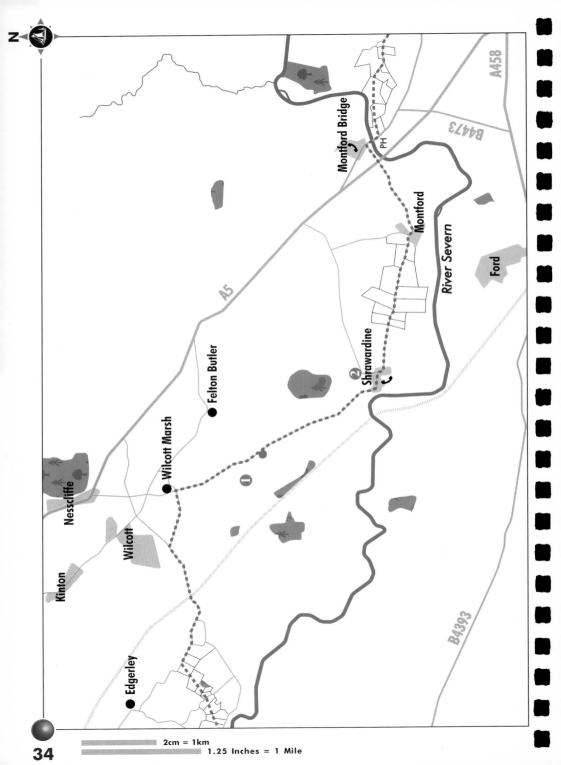

N

Montford Bridge

PH

Montford

River Severn

Ford

A458

B4473

A5

Felton Butler

Shrawardine

Wilcott Marsh

Nesscliffe

Wilcott

Kinton

B4393

Edgerley

2cm = 1km
1.25 Inches = 1 Mile

Continue down the road to Wilcott Marsh, turning right at a crossroads and walking towards Shrawardine. The area to your right is farmland, but is used for military training. During the Second World War the Central Ammunition Storage Depot ❶ was sited here and the storage sheds, buffered by earth embankments, still stand. Fortunately, they are scattered and relatively well-concealed, making only a limited impact on the landscape.

SHRAWARDINE

As you continue along the lane you will pass a house named Shrawardine Castle, but the original castle is in the village, a little further on. Shrawardine (locals call it Shraden) is an attractive place with timber-framed cottages and a sandstone church, St Mary's, which is partly Norman, though much restored and rebuilt. Shrawardine Castle ❷ now consists only of a mound, part of a ditch and fragments of masonry in a field on the east side of the village. The earliest castle on this site was probably built soon after the Conquest by Rainald the Sheriff, whom Domesday Book records as holding the manor of Shrawardine. It later became a Royal castle, serving as an outpost of Shrewsbury, and was destroyed by the Welsh in 1215. It was rebuilt after 1220 and what survives today is from that period. The castle was dismantled by Cromwell's troops in 1645, after a siege lasting just five days. Much of the stone was used for repairs to Shrewsbury Castle.

Having passed Shrawardine Church, you reach a junction. If you wish to visit the castle remains, turn left, then right on a footpath. But to continue the Severn Way turn right (signposted 'No Through Road'), and shortly follow the road round as it bends to the left. Keep on to the end of the hard surfacing, and then go forward onto a green lane that guides you into Montford, just by St Chad's Church.

MONTFORD

This small, quiet hamlet once formed part of the huge Powis Estate (based on Powis Castle at Welshpool). The square-towered, sandstone church occupies a dominant position on high ground above the river, with fine views to the Breidden Hills. It's a relatively recent building, dating from 1737-8, and was designed by a Shrewsbury man, William Cooper.

Just outside the church is the grave of Charles Darwin's parents. His father, Robert, was the son of Erasmus Darwin, a prominent physician, poet and freethinker who anticipated his grandson's views on evolution. Charles's mother, Sussanah, was the daughter of Josiah Wedgwood, the potter.

Pass the church and continue along the lane, which takes you over the A5 to reach a crossroads at the riverside settlement of Montford Bridge.

A bridge has spanned the Severn here since the early Middle Ages but the present one was built in 1792 by Thomas Telford. This ancient river crossing was once a traditional meeting place for negotiations between English and Welsh leaders in times of conflict. In 1283 Dafydd ap Gruffudd, the last true Prince of Wales, was brought here in chains by his own countrymen and handed over to the English. He was tried for treason at a Parliament (claimed to be the first full English Parliament) called by Edward I and held at Acton Burnell, south of Shrewsbury. Dafydd was convicted and subsequently dragged through the streets of Shrewsbury, tied to a horse's tail, before being hung, drawn and quartered.

Purple loosestrife - a common riverside plant

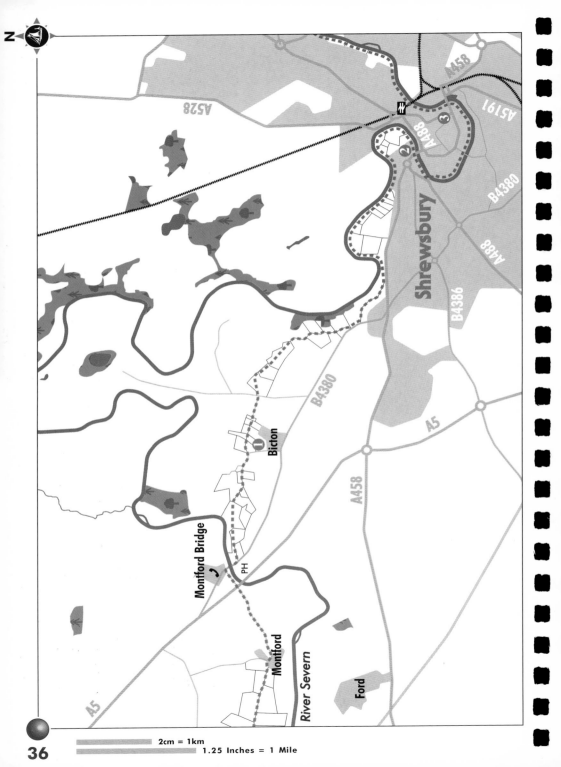

N

Shrewsbury

A528
A458
A5191
A488
B4380
A488
B4386
B4380
A5
A458

Bicton

Montford Bridge
PH
Montford
Ford
River Severn

A5

2cm = 1km
1.25 Inches = 1 Mile

NTO SHREWSBURY

Between Montford Bridge and the outskirts of Shrewsbury you will see nothing of the Severn, which loops northwards in a convoluted fashion that would have added 13km (8 miles) to the walk were you able to follow it. Instead, you get farmlands and hedgerows below buzzard-patrolled skies.

Turn right at the crossroads in Montford Bridge, cross the Severn and, just opposite the Wingfield Arms, turn left onto a track between houses. Go through two gates and alongside a fence to a footbridge. Cross one field and then, in the next, go forward by a fence to pass through a gate at the top. Follow a hedgerow round to two more gates and take the right-hand one.

Follow a green track between hedgerows to a farm track that leads to a road. Turn right into Bicton, passing an old yew-shrouded churchyard enclosing the scant ruins of a 16th-century church ❶ next to Bicton Hall. A cluster of cottages and farms completes the hamlet, often known as Old Bicton to distinguish it from the modern village, which has grown up nearby around a church built in 1885.

Stay on the road until it bends to the right. Leave it here, on the left go through a gate and follow a track to Grove Farm, beyond which a lane leads to a T-junction. Cross the road and join a path to the right of Rossall Lodge, going over two stiles before striking across a field. On the other side go through two bridle gates, and forward alongside a fence, following the headland across two fields. On the far side you reach a field-edge track, but soon leave it, on the left, through a gate, continuing alongside a fence at the edge of a large open pasture, to a stile in a corner. Beyond the stile go forward between hedgerows to join an access track.

When you come out to a road at Shelton turn left, and soon left again, on a bridleway that descends as a broad track into woodland, before continuing as a holloway, eventually to meet a rising gravel track. At the top of the track, a stile gives onto an overgrown footpath between a hedgerow and a fence by an adjoining service road. At the top end of the road and footpath you reach a fine viewpoint over the Severn. Steps descend towards the riverbank, which is now followed to the outskirts of Shrewsbury.

At the end of a large field the riverside path runs between two fences, and ends by climbing steps, at the top of which you turn left onto a walled path bordered by houses. When you reach another flight of steps

descend to follow a path at the rear of gardens, to a stile, and later rising into a large open field. Continue along the riverbank to an isolated waymark post. Turn sharp right to a stile by a stand of willows, and onto a path into a playing field.

Turn left round the field edge, and gradually drift back to the Severn. Pass under Frankwell Footbridge to the edge of a car park and continue by the river to pass under Welsh Bridge ❷, built in its present form in 1795, though there was a bridge here soon after 1100. The riverside path eventually leads up Water Lane to a road. Turn left, go past the Boathouse Inn, and then left over Port Hill Bridge, a handsome suspension bridge of 1922. On the other side turn right and follow the river, passing under Kingsland Bridge and Greyfriars Bridge before reaching English Bridge ❸, built in 1774, and rebuilt in 1925, though the Severn was first spanned here c1100.

English Bridge, Shrewsbury

Milk Street in Shrewsbury

IT was the River Severn that determined Shrewsbury's siting, its development and, to a large extent, its present character. The Saxon town of Scrobbesbyrig was built within the natural moat provided by a tight loop of the Severn, completely encircled except for a small gap, making a perfect defensive site. Even the gap was guarded by a ridge, on which a castle was later built.

Soon after the Norman Conquest, King William gave much of Shropshire to Roger de Montgomery, creating him Earl of Shrewsbury. Roger built a substantial castle and for many years the town was a base for Norman operations against the Welsh. At the same time, however, it was building on its riverside location to become a busy inland port. By the 14th century, despite involvement in border conflicts, it was one of the wealthiest towns in England, successful in a variety of trades. It was the woollen cloth trade, however, which assumed pre-eminence and it remained Shrewsbury's staple until the end of the 18th century, reaching its peak in the Tudor period, after peace with Wales had finally been achieved. It was the wool merchants and drapers who built many of the spectacular timber-framed mansions which still grace Shrewsbury's streets today.

Following the disruption of the Civil War, and a gradual decline in the wool trade, Shrewsbury became a fashionable centre for leisure and shopping, a role which expanded in the great coaching era, thanks to the town's position on the main London-Holyhead road. The coming of the railways killed both road and river traffic but opened up new opportunities. With the subsequent decline of the railways, Shrewsbury has fallen prey to the usual traffic congestion, but remains an important regional centre. For today's visitor, much of its charm derives from the survival of its medieval street pattern, particularly the abundance of narrow passages known locally as shuts and gullets. There's a great deal to see, with a total of 660 Listed Buildings in the town centre alone. Few places have such an astonishing wealth of period buildings and the impact is all the greater because most are crowded together in the centre, within the Severn's tight embrace.

The best way to get to grips with all this is to begin with a visit to the Tourist Information Centre, housed in the Music Hall, an imposing building in The Square at the centre of town. You can buy a very useful leaflet here describing a town trail, as well as a good range of other leaflets and books. One of Shrewsbury's most interesting buildings is right opposite the TIC - this is the Market Hall, built in 1596 for the sale of woollen cloth, and a great many other fine buildings are just round the corner on High Street.

There is no room here for an exhaustive list of Shrewsbury's attractions, but a few highlights might include its medieval churches, the best of which is St Mary's, a mixture of many periods, but originally a Saxon foundation. The ancient centre of Shrewsbury is St Alkmund's Square, where there are two churches of Saxon origin, both rebuilt in the 18th century: St Julian's, which now houses a craft centre, and St Alkmund's itself. The peaceful oasis of Belmont contains the ruins of Old St Chad's, while the Abbey Church, founded in 1083 by Roger de Montgomery, is just beyond English Bridge.

One of Shrewsbury's most famous sons is, of course, Charles Darwin, who attended Shrewsbury School, a superb building founded by Edward VI in 1552. Darwin's statue sits outside it, but it is now Shrewsbury Library, the school having moved across the river to Kingsland in 1882. Almost opposite the library is one of the finest of all provincial railway stations, a masterpiece of Victorian "Tudor". Nearby is the castle - not Roger de Montgomery's original but a later one, remodelled by Thomas Telford.

Other notable buildings include Bear Steps, the Council House Gatehouse, Abbot's House, Ireland's Mansion, Owen's Mansion and Rowley's House. Some of the finest streets are Butcher Row, Dogpole, Wyle Cop, Claremont Hill, High Street, Fish Street and Milk Street. But this is only to scratch the surface, and wherever you look you will find much of interest.

It's also worth noting that Shrewsbury has excellent public transport links and a wide range of all facilities, including probably a better selection of tempting places to eat and drink than almost any town of comparable size.

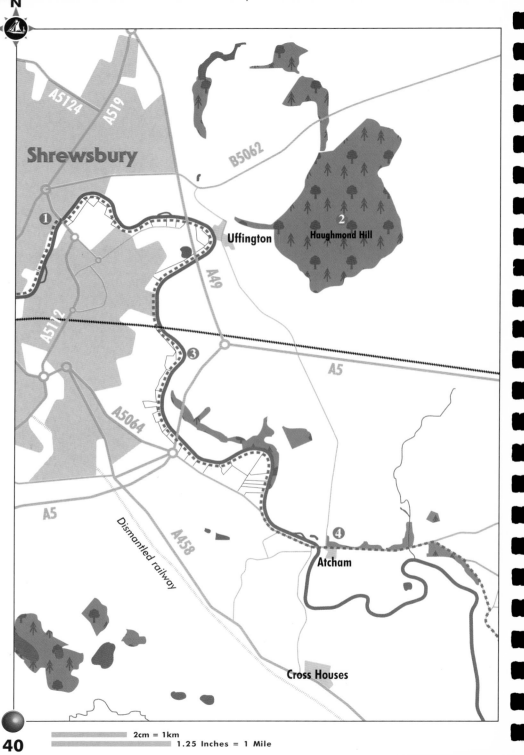

N

Shrewsbury

A5124

A519

B5062

①

A5112

Uffington

Haughmond Hill

2

A49

③

A5

A5064

A5

Dismantled railway

A458

Atcham

④

Cross Houses

2cm = 1km
1.25 Inches = 1 Mile

Continue under English Bridge, and on to pass below the railway, following a riverside towpath to a road, near a weir. Keep ahead and when the road bends left stay on a narrow stony path beside the river. At the bridge linking Ditherington to Monkmoor ❶, climb steps and cross the bridge, descending on the other side to join a path along the true right bank of the river as it meanders onwards past Monkmoor, eventually passing below the A49.

UFFINGTON

The village of Uffington comes into view on the far bank, but the ferry which once connected Uffington to the Monkmoor side of the river no longer operates. Monkmoor is where the war poet Wilfred Owen lived as a boy in the early years of the 20th century. He and his family enjoyed Sunday walks by the Severn and would often take the ferry over to Uffington to attend services at the village church. Beyond Uffington rises flat-topped Haughmond Hill ❷, covered in Forestry Commission plantations and a popular place for walks and picnics.

The riverside path again passes under the A49, and continues to the edge of the Monkmoor housing estates. Just a little further on you come into a large field with a pylon in it. Go round the field edge to the far corner, emerging briefly onto an estate road. A few strides later bear left to return to the Severn, continuing on a narrow path by the river, and crossing a short stretch of boardwalk.

Go under the impressive Belvidere Bridge, which carries the Shrewsbury-Birmingham railway across the Severn. At nearby Preston Boats ❸ a rope ferry used to operate above an old fish weir originally owned by Haughmond Abbey.

The path passes into light woodland. When it forks, branch left, staying by the river. Emerging from the woodland, press on to eventually pass beneath the A5. Shortly afterwards the Wrekin comes into view ahead. Continue past Emstrey Farm and soon rejoin a riverside path, which finally meets the B4380 at a stile. Turn left to Atcham.

ATCHAM

Atcham is a small village distinguished by the presence of Attingham Park ❹, a National Trust property which was built to the design of George Stuart in 1783-5 for Noel Hill, first Lord Berwick. One of Shropshire's grandest houses, it has a magnificent Regency interior and is surrounded by parkland landscaped by the renowned Humphrey Repton.

On a much more human scale, however, is St Eata's Church, which stands by the Severn. It was first built in the 11th century, though what remains is mostly of later construction. It is the only church in Britain dedicated to the Celtic St Eata, who was consecrated Bishop of Lindisfarne in AD678. Much of the north wall is of Saxon construction, built with stones brought from the Roman town of Viroconium.

Close to the church is a handsome Georgian pub, the Mermaid, formerly the Mytton and Mermaid (the notorious Jack Mytton was one of Shropshire's more colourful characters), and there are some interesting cottages in the village. There are also two bridges spanning the Severn. The good-looking but redundant one was built in the 1770s by John Gwynn, the Shrewsbury architect who also designed English Bridge, the famous Magdalen Bridge at Oxford and Worcester Bridge, which you will cross in a few days' time as you head south on the Severn Way. The other bridge was built in the 1920s.

The Council House Gatehouse on Castle Street, Shrewsbury

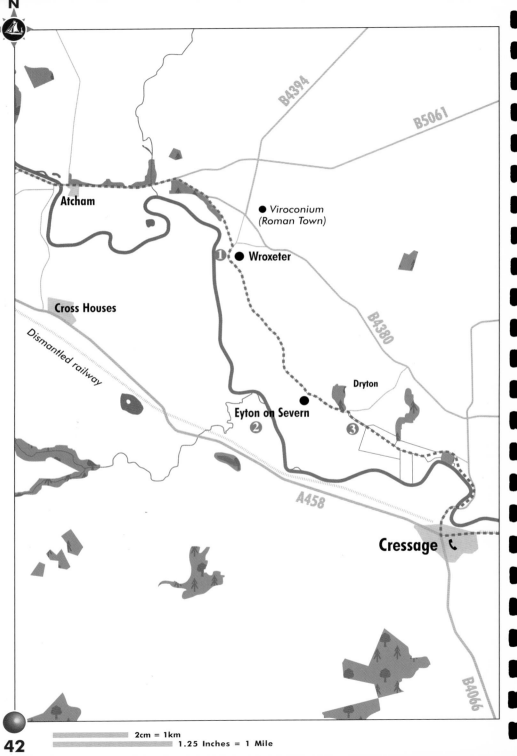

N

Atcham

● Viroconium
(Roman Town)

① ● Wroxeter

Cross Houses

Dismantled railway

Dryton

Eyton on Severn
②

③

A458

Cressage 📞

B4394

B5061

B4380

B4066

2cm = 1km
1.25 Inches = 1 Mile

Between Atcham and Cressage the Severn Way almost entirely follows roads. Most are quiet, pleasant and relatively traffic-free, but care needs to be taken against approaching vehicles. Although the route bypasses it, a short detour to the Roman town of Viroconium is worthwhile.

From Atcham, continue along the B4380, which branches right soon after crossing the River Tern. About 500m/yds later turn right again onto a narrow lane that leads to a T-junction on the edge of Wroxeter. A right turn takes you through the village and on along the Severn Way. However, turn left, and then left again, if you wish to visit Viroconium.

VIROCONIUM

The remains of Viroconium are in the care of English Heritage and open to the public. The excavated site is relatively small but, at its zenith, Viroconium was the fourth largest Roman town in Britain. It began as a military camp cAD58 but when the legion was moved to Chester about 30 years later the site was developed as a civil town. Most of the visible remains are of the 2nd-century municipal baths, but the size of these gives an indication of the scale of the town. Also uncovered are parts of the exercise hall, market hall and forum. Still standing is an impressive section of a basilica wall, known as the "Old Work". Aerial photography has demonstrated, by means of crop marks, the presence of streets, houses and fortifications beneath the surface of the surrounding farmland. After the Romans left it seems that urban life continued at Viroconium until perhaps the 7th century, but it was eventually abandoned and regarded only as a useful source of building stone.

Return to Wroxeter, where St Andrew's Church ❶ is also of interest. Part of the nave is Saxon and was built with stone from Viroconium. The font is believed to be made from part of a Roman column and the churchyard gateposts are Roman too. There are some attractive houses in the village, and earthworks in the neighbouring fields are part of Viroconium's defences.

Follow the road south from Wroxeter, passing through the hamlet of Eyton on Severn ❷, where there stands an unusual tower, all that remains of the demolished Eyton Hall, the birthplace of the poet, philosopher and diplomat Edward Herbert (1583-1648). Approaching another hamlet, Lower Dryton, leave the lane at a gate, branching right onto a wide

track, which runs down into the edge of a large arable field. To your right is the unexpected sight of a National Hunt Racecourse ❸.

Turn left across two fields. About 200m/yds into the second field, go left through a hedgerow and over a stile. In the ensuing pasture, turn right alongside a fence, and then bear left on a narrow path, climbing past a mid-field oak to a waymark post on a small rise. From the waymark, cross to the corner of the field, at the left-hand edge of woodland.

Follow a track to the far side of the woodland then turn right and diagonally cross an arable field, aiming for the left edge of the woodland boundary ahead. Reaching a stile, cross it and turn left through scrub. On the far side you emerge into a long, narrow riverside field and can follow the Severn to Cressage Bridge. Cross the bridge and walk up to a road junction near the war memorial in Cressage.

The Basilica at Viroconium Roman Town, Wroxeter

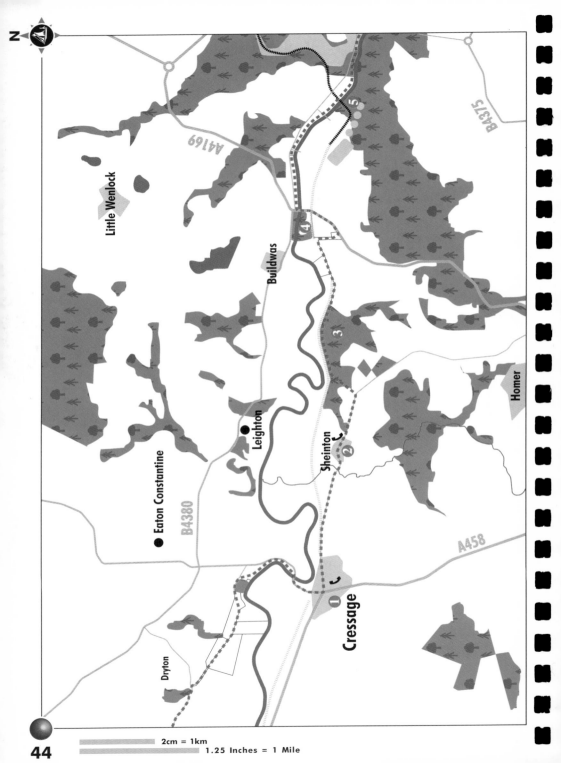

N

Little Wenlock

Buildwas

A4169

B4375

Eaton Constantine

B4380

Leighton

Sheinton

Homer

A458

Cressage

Dryton

44

2cm = 1km
1.25 Inches = 1 Mile

More road walking takes the Way on as far as Sheinton, beyond which peaceful woodland and farmland pastures lead you towards the magnificent abbey ruins at Buildwas. After that the former industrial town of Ironbridge awaits, reached by mainly riverside paths dominated by Buildwas Power Station.

The village of Cressage ❶ has a useful pub and village stores. It is claimed that the Pope's emissary St Augustine preached to the Welsh bishops in AD584 under the Cressage Oak (originally Christ's Oak, from which the village name derives) which stood for centuries on the site now occupied by the war memorial.

At the war memorial, turn left on the road to Sheinton. Pass Sheinton Church❷, perched above the road, as you climb eastwards out of the village. Almost a kilometre (about half a mile) further on, as the road bends gently to the right, leave it, going left down a driveway to Buildwas Park. Just as you reach a house, leave the driveway and cross a nearby stile to descend into the delightful mixed woodland of Piner's Coppice ❸. At the end of the woodland, climb past Park Farm and head along a rough-surfaced track that eventually passes Mill Farm to meet the A4169. Turn left, soon passing Buildwas Abbey ❹.

BUILDWAS ABBEY

Another English Heritage property, this Cistercian abbey was founded in 1135 as a daughter house of Furness Abbey in Cumbria. The surviving buildings date from c1200 and the most substantial remains are of the church, famous for its superb nave arcades, and the chapter house, with its fine vaulted roof.

The abbey owned many outlying farms and even had its own ironworks, a precursor of the later industrial development at Coalbrookdale and Ironbridge.

Cross Buildwas Bridge and turn right towards Ironbridge. After 150m/yds leave the road, at a stile beside a gate, entering a riverside meadow. Follow the riverbank to a path that wanders through woodland. Go under a bridge, still following a riverside path until it meets a road. Turn right for 100m/yds, and go back through a hedgerow to continue by the river.

Eventually you reach a paved walkway and pass beneath the impressive Albert Edward Bridge ❺, built by John Fowler in 1863. Today it carries only coal trains fuelling the power station. Pass Ironbridge Rowing Club to enter Dale End Riverside Park. When you reach the Ironbridge Antiques Centre turn left to the main road, and then right to walk into Ironbridge.

IRONBRIDGE

It was at Coalbrookdale in 1709 that Abraham Darby discovered that coke could be used instead of charcoal for smelting iron. It sounds a small thing but it sparked a revolution that changed the world. Suddenly, iron could be made cheaply in large quantities, instead of being dependent on the slow, laborious process of charcoal production. It was Darby's grandson, Abraham III, who constructed the world's first iron bridge. Cast in 1779, it still spans the Severn just south of Coalbrookdale, at the place now known to the world as Ironbridge.

For a time the Ironbridge Gorge was the world's foremost industrial centre until it declined in the face of competition from the Black Country and South Wales. The industrial scars have healed and the gorge is green once more, but since the 1960s those industrial relics which do survive have been transformed into a collection of fascinating museums, and Ironbridge is now a UNESCO-designated World Heritage Site.

Buildwas Abbey

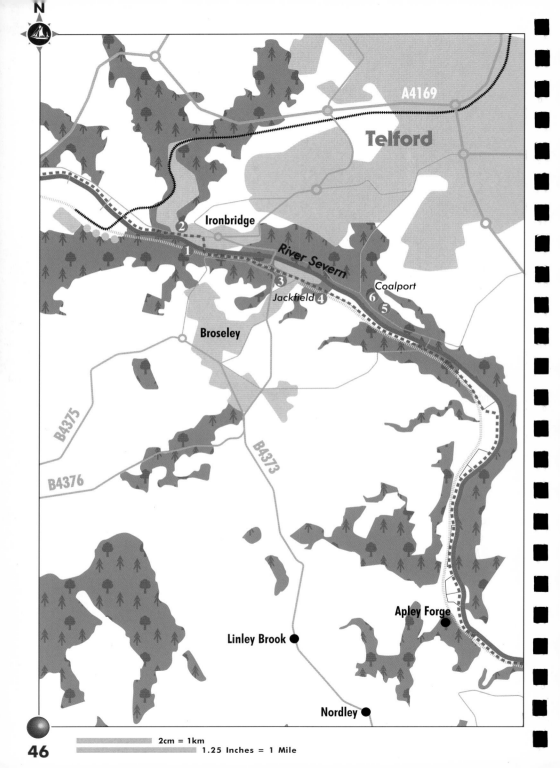

N

A4169

Telford

② Ironbridge

River Severn

③
Jackfield ④ Coalport ⑥ ⑤

①

Broseley

B4375

B4373

B4376

Linley Brook ●

Apley Forge ●

Nordley ●

46

2cm = 1km
1.25 Inches = 1 Mile

JACKFIELD

It's worth exploring Ironbridge before you leave, even if you don't intend to visit the museums (it takes a few days to do justice to all of them). Despite its popularity as a tourist destination, Ironbridge remains unspoilt, its mellow brick houses clinging in tiers to the steep north side of the gorge, high above the thickly wooded riverbank. The actual Iron Bridge ❶ is a graceful structure and the focal point of the little town. A tollhouse at its southern end serves as an information centre, while the main Tourist Information Centre ❷ is across the river on The Wharfage.

When you're ready to leave, cross the Iron Bridge and turn left through the car park that has replaced the railway station. On the far side join the former railway trackbed, walking through pleasant mixed woodland. The railway was, of course, the Severn Valley line, which ran from Shrewsbury to Hartlebury (near Stourport).

When you reach a road at an old level crossing gate (said to be the widest in Britain) keep right and continue into Church Road. Go past the Jackfield Tile Museum ❸ and the church of St Mary the Virgin. As the road surfacing ends go down a stony track to the riverbank and onto a path rising through scrubby woodland. Meeting a lane at a U-bend, go left towards a former pub, but keep to the right of it on a tarmac path which brings you out at Maws Craft Centre ❹, housed in the surviving buildings of what was once the largest encaustic tileworks in the world. Keep forward alongside the centre and on into Ferry Road, passing terraced cottages, the Boat Inn (note the flood levels marked on its door) and the War Memorial Bridge.

COALPORT

A short detour across the footbridge takes you into Coalport, where facilities include a seasonal tea shop, pubs and a youth hostel. There is much of historical interest here, including Coalport China Museum ❺, next to which a stop lock and a short stretch of water are all that remain of the Coalport section of the Shropshire Canal, built 1788-92 by ironmaster William Reynolds to link local mines and ironworks with the Severn. Close to the footbridge is the Hay Inclined Plane, a major industrial monument and now part of the acclaimed Blists Hill Museum ❻. It was the means by which boats were transferred between canals - they were carried up and down the

1-in-3 gradient on wheeled cradles. Nearby is another fascinating industrial site, the Tar Tunnel.

Just past the Boat Inn follow the road as it rises to the right, and pass under the former railway, then turn left up steps to the trackbed, and turn right. Eventually the route is deflected left by a couple of cottages, descending to a riverside path, which later leads through Preen's Eddy Picnic Area to a road at Coalport Bridge, near the Woodbridge Inn (Coalport Bridge, now cast iron, was originally wooden).

Turn right, walking up the road to the old station, then turning left along a concrete-surfaced lane (the course of the dismantled railway) as far as a Severn Trent waterworks, just beyond which you branch left on a track descending to meet the riverbank once more, at Foundry Cottage (the site of a former ironworks). Beyond, continue along the riverside path, passing briefly in and out of woodland, and on to Apley Forge and its elegant footbridge.

The Iron Bridge

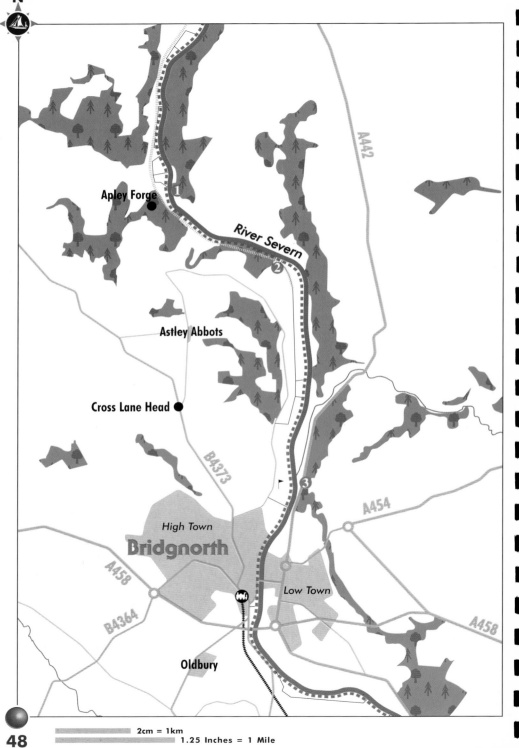

N

Apley Forge

River Severn

A442

Astley Abbots

Cross Lane Head

B4373

High Town

Bridgnorth

Low Town

A454

A458

B4364

Oldbury

A458

2cm = 1km
1.25 Inches = 1 Mile

Between Apley Forge and Bridgnorth the route hugs the riverbank, and provides easy walking along a pleasant, peaceful and particularly well-wooded stretch of the Severn. Kingfishers and grey wagtails frequent the river and cormorants are present in autumn and winter.

APLEY

There are just a few Victorian cottages at Apley Forge today and it's hard to imagine that this sublimely peaceful place was once the scene of industry, with two forges in operation (the site of Upper Forge is just a short distance away, a little further up Linley Brook). The surrounding woods - Rookery Coppice, The Boat Coppice and Chestnut Coppice - were formerly harvested to provide sustainable supplies of fuel for the forges. The practice of coppicing (cutting trees to ground level on a regular cycle of around 10 years) ensures a continual crop of small timber. Just a little way downstream are the remains of wharves on the riverbank, which must have served the forge.

Across the river, set in beautiful Apley Park, below the steep, wooded cliffs of Apley Terrace, stands Apley Hall, which was until recently used as a school and is now a retirement home. A large, castellated, Gothic mansion of Grinshill stone, it was built for Bridgnorth MP Thomas Whitmore in 1811, incorporating an older Georgian house, which itself stood on the site of a house built in 1308. A handsome, white-painted suspension bridge ❶ built soon after 1900 spans the river, and was built to link Apley Park with Linley Station on the Severn Valley Railway. The bridge is private, providing no public access to the east bank. The former station house is just to the north of Apley Forge. When the railway was in operation Linley used to be a frequent winner in competitions for the best kept station.

Continuing south beside the Severn there is one point where a slight detour is helpful to avoid a difficult stretch of the riverside path. The detour is not a right of way but appears to be an acceptable diversion.

Beyond Chestnut Coppice you pass some rock houses ❷ hollowed out of a small sandstone bluff. The sandstone in this area, and downstream almost as far as Worcester, lends itself to this treatment and you will see plenty more such man-made caves, many of which were lived in until comparatively recently, even, in some cases, into the 1960s.

Approaching Bridgnorth, the route runs along the edge of a golf course, while the far bank rises to sheer, pine-clad, sandstone cliffs. Just outside the town, High Rock and Pendlestone Rock ❸ are particularly impressive. Below the latter look out for bizarre Fort Pendlestone. Rebuilt in its present form by William Whitmore of Apley Hall in the 19th century, it has had many uses, including an industrial estate.

Reaching the edge of town, you join a road and continue in front of new houses built on the site of a medieval friary established by the Franciscan Order between 1224 and 1244. Documentary evidence shows that both Henry III and Edward I contributed towards the building costs. The friary was closed in 1538 during the Dissolution of the Monasteries but it was only in the 19th century that it was demolished. Only the slightest of remains survive today.

Continue to the end of Riverside, and turn up to a junction. Go left to reach the main road bridge spanning the Severn.

Young fronds of male fern unfurling

Bishop Percy's House on Cartway, Bridgnorth

THE most dramatic of the Severnside towns, Bridgnorth is quite unlike anywhere else in Britain and often comes as a surprise to those seeing it for the first time because of the almost continental way it clings to the top of a high sandstone cliff. There are more surprises in store for those who take the time to explore it fully and the first port of call should be the Tourist Information Centre in Listley Street, where details are available of all the varied attractions and facilities on offer.

It was in 912 that King Alfred's daughter, Ethelfleda, built a fortified township above the Severn, a township that was later to grow into Bridgnorth as we know it today. It was an obviously strategic position, and, as a centre of communications, a river crossing and a port, Bridgnorth was well placed to prosper. By the 13th century, the only Shropshire town greater in importance was Shrewsbury, though Bridgnorth was a busier port. There were three dockyards in the town and numerous boats were built in them, while as a flourishing port Bridgnorth naturally attracted industry, particularly ironworks and carpet mills, as well as brewing, tanning and a variety of other trades.

By the 19th century, Bridgnorth was declining as an industrial centre and when the Severn Valley Railway opened in 1862, linking Shrewsbury with Worcester, it spelt the end for the river trade. Only a century later the railway was itself closed, but fortunately a preservation society was formed and steam trains now regularly run between Bridgnorth and Kidderminster, contributing significantly to the tourist trade which is a vital part of Bridgnorth's economy today.

Bridgnorth is actually two towns: High Town, which crowns the sandstone cliff and clings to its sides; and Low Town, which occupies the riverside below and the east bank. A road links the two, with further pedestrian access provided by seven ancient stairways and a cartway cut into the sandstone. A remarkable cliff railway, opened in 1892 and now the only inland cliff railway in Britain, provides an alternative route.

Low Town is neglected by visitors to Bridgnorth, but is full of interest in its own right, with some charming buildings and a good view of High Town from the bridge which spans the Severn. A notable event, which took place just upstream, was the construction in 1808 of the world's first passenger steam locomotive, designed by Richard Trevithick and made by John Rastrick at Hazledine's Foundry.

But it's High Town which has the most to offer, including the remains of a castle, originally built by Robert de Belleme, the son of Roger de Montgomery, in 1101-2, though the keep was built by Henry II about 60 years later. The castle was surrendered by its Royalist garrison to Cromwell in 1646 during the Civil War, and subsequently dismantled. All that remains is the keep, tilted at a crazy angle three times greater than the Leaning Tower of Pisa.

Castle Walk provides a fine view - in fact Charles I in 1642 called it the finest in his kingdom. Neighbouring East Castle Street is one of Bridgnorth's most elegant thoroughfares, with gracious Georgian buildings leading the eye to the classical-style Church of St Mary Magdalene, built in 1792 to the design of Thomas Telford.

The original parish church is St Leonard's, at the other end of town, a commanding edifice of dark red sandstone, which stands in a calm little oasis of period buildings. Steps descend from the church to the river, but of the ancient staircases and passageways linking the cliff-top with the riverside, it is Cartway that is the best known. For centuries, it was the main route out of High Town and today it is still lined with attractive buildings, most notable of which is the gabled, timber-framed Bishop Percy's House, dated 1580. Several of Cartway's houses have heavy wooden shutters, designed for protection from the jostling of carts, wagons and horses. There are caves in the sandstone, which were used as homes until 1856, and there are more by the riverside, formerly used for storage as well as habitation.

Other highlights of Bridgnorth include the former Town Hall (1650-52), Waterloo Terrace, Stoneway Steps, and the railway station, now the northern terminus of the Severn Valley Railway. Like most Shropshire towns, however, its greatest charm lies probably in its harmonious and unpretentious mix of architectural styles, best appreciated in a leisurely walk around its endlessly fascinating streets.

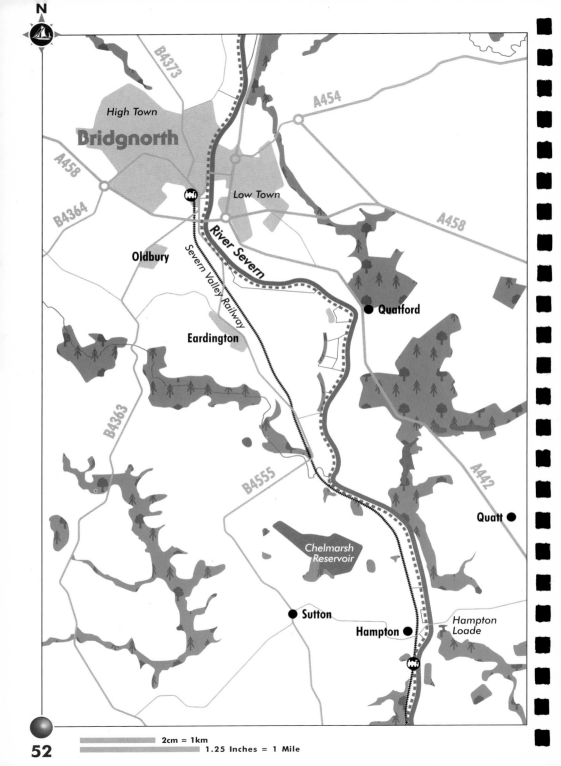

N

High Town

Bridgnorth

A454

Low Town

A458

A458

B4373

B4364

Oldbury

River Severn

Severn Valley Railway

Eardington

Quatford

B4363

A442

B4555

Quatt

Chelmarsh
Reservoir

Sutton

Hampton
Loade

Hampton

2cm = 1km

1.25 Inches = 1 Mile

Between Bridgnorth and Hampton the Severn Way simply follows the river, mainly through waterside pastures. This is delightful and easy walking, with the Severn Valley Railway for company. The railway stations at Bridgnorth and Hampton are both worth a visit.

At the bridge, cross the road and descend to a paved area, going forward onto a narrow path that later moves into adjoining riverside fields, with steep, tree-clad cliffs rising to your right. In recent years, many more trees, including wild cherries, have been planted at the foot of the cliffs. The river, however, is bordered mainly by alders and willows - trees that are tolerant of flooding.

Just opposite Quatford, at a field edge, you go back to the riverside path. Quatford was once the site of a camp established by Danish invaders in 893, and the Norman Earl of Shrewsbury, Roger de Montgomery, later built a settlement on the site in the 1070s. The earthworks of his castle still stand by the river and some Norman work survives in the church. Roger's son, Robert de Belleme, transferred the settlement to a more easily defended site upstream, which we now know as Bridgnorth.

When the path meets buildings at Lower Forge, once the site of an ironworks which specialised in nail-making, keep left beside the river, shortly branching left again onto a narrow riverside path. After crossing a tributary, Mor Brook, the path runs close to the railway.

THE SEVERN VALLEY RAILWAY

The SVR is the most popular preserved line in the country, with a large number of beautifully restored locomotives and carriages operating on a delightful route between Bridgnorth and Kidderminster. Trains run throughout the year though to a much-reduced timetable in winter. From May to October, however, there are frequent services and the line is probably busier now than at any time in its history.

Easy walking along the edge of riverside pastures leads you past the grounds of Dudmaston Hall, on the far bank. The Dudmaston Estate has remained in the same family for 850 years, though it was given to the National Trust in 1978. Because it is still lived in, the Hall has a warmer, more intimate feel than many National Trust properties, but it is for its beautiful grounds that Dudmaston is most famous, with woodland, parkland and tree-fringed lakes.

Soon after leaving Dudmaston behind, a South Staffs Waterworks footbridge (no public access) is passed before the Way goes swiftly on to Hampton. Facilities at Hampton include the Unicorn Inn, seasonal refreshments at the railway station, a telephone and a cable ferry to Hampton Loade (the last working ferry on the Severn, except for the seasonal Cathedral Ferry at Worcester).

HAMPTON

The village is just a few cottages, chalets and caravans. The station, however, merits the short detour. Great wicker baskets of damsons used to be loaded onto the trains here and transported to Manchester to be made into dyes for the cotton trade. Those days may be long gone, but something of their atmosphere remains and Hampton Station has featured in many period films. Across the river is Hampton Loade, the second part of its name derived from a Saxon word usually taken to mean a ford. From 1796 until 1866, there were forges at Hampton Loade where Papermill Brook joins the Severn, but today it is a popular spot with anglers, walkers and picnickers.

The Cliff Railway, Bridgnorth

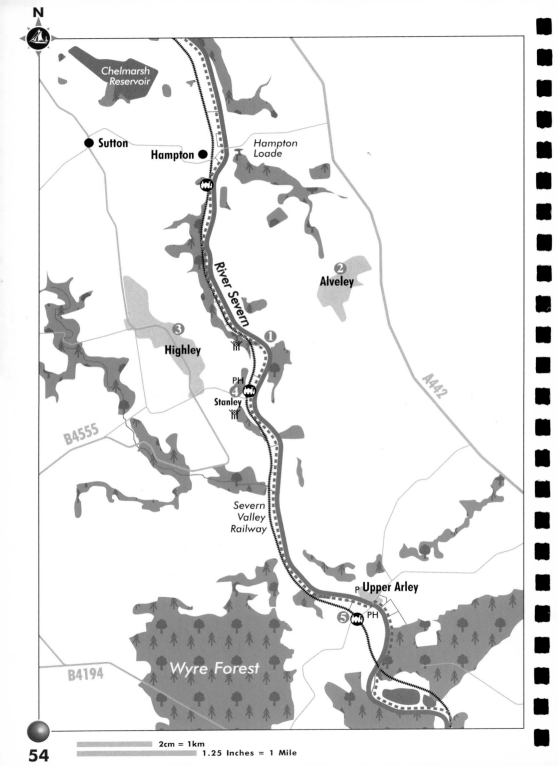

N

Chelmarsh
Reservoir

● Sutton

Hampton ●

Hampton
Loade

River Severn

② Alveley

③ Highley

①

PH
④

Stanley

Severn
Valley
Railway

A442

B4555

Wyre Forest

B4194

P ⑤ PH Upper Arley

2cm = 1km
1.25 Inches = 1 Mile

From Hampton to Upper Arley, the Severn Way continues to follow the river closely, either through riverside pastures or in flanking mixed woodland. The walking is nowhere difficult, and everywhere a delight.

Having walked past the ferry, bear left to the water's edge and enter a large riverside field. With little deviation, the route continues through peaceful countryside to reach a country park on the edge of Highley.

SEVERN VALLEY COUNTRY PARK

The country park straddles the river, including land at both Highley (west bank) and Alveley (east bank), linked by a footbridge, the Miners' Bridge. Both Highley and Alveley were once mining and quarrying centres at the northern limit of the Wyre Forest coalfield. Quarrying, in particular, has a long history here; it is believed that some of the stone for Worcester Cathedral came from Highley and was sent downstream by boat. Coalmining began in the Middle Ages, but remained small-scale until the 19th century. Production peaked between 1879 and 1969 and the Miners' Bridge was built both for the convenience of the workers and to bring coal from the east bank to the railway on the west bank.

The quarries had been more or less worked out by 1912, but it was 1969 before the last colliery closed, leaving a scarred landscape full of spoil heaps. Natural regeneration began at once, especially on the west bank, with alder, ash, rowan, birch and hazel having little difficulty in recolonising the fertile soils. However, a helping hand was also given, and since 1988 the former industrial sites have been transformed, with the planting of thousands of trees, mostly native species, and the creation of ponds and meadows. There is a visitor centre ❶ on the east bank. Just beyond it, the village of Alveley ❷ has attractive cottages, a 12th-century church, and what is claimed to be Shropshire's oldest pub.

When you reach the Miners' Bridge, you can either go forward beneath the bridge, or up steps to access Highley (pubs and shops) or cross the bridge to the visitor centre and/or Alveley. The village of Highley ❸ is about ten minutes walk away, but contains little other than a Norman church and an adjacent timber-framed house, though it is a particularly good example of an Edwardian mining village. The riverside path contiues to a small settlement, Stanley, next to Highley station ❹ which is only a short distance from the riverside.

S̶TANLEY

This was a busy place for centuries, long before the railway was built, with barge traffic carrying coal, stone and timber. The Ship Inn was licensed in 1770, and originally catered for bargees, miners and quarrymen. Today, it's popular with walkers, anglers and railway enthusiasts. For many of the latter, Highley Station is the finest on the SVR, with its evocative ticket office and waiting room and flower-filled platform. Even the public toilets recall a more gracious age.

The Severn Way goes on past Stanley as a broad, rough-surfaced access track. When you reach a junction, turn left on a descending gravel track back to the riverside, where a stile gives onto a path.

Delightful walking between river and railway now guides you towards Upper Arley, the first Worcestershire village on the Way. The parish is divided by the Severn, with the Harbour Inn and Arley Station ❺ on the west bank. The station (seasonal refreshments available) is another gem, and has featured in films and TV programmes, including the recent BBC comedy series Oh! Dr Beeching!

Hampton Loade Ferry

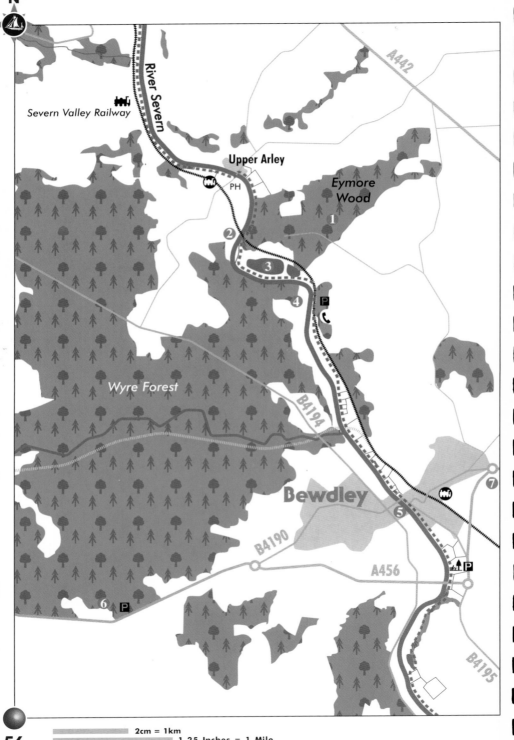

N

Severn Valley Railway

River Severn

Upper Arley

PH

Eymore Wood

1

2

3

4

P

Wyre Forest

B4194

Bewdley

5

7

6

P

B4190

A456

A442

B4195

P

2cm = 1km
1.25 Inches = 1 Mile

At Upper Arley the route crosses a footbridge to the other side of the Severn and merges with the Worcestershire Way for a short distance. Before heading south, however, you may want to explore this charming village. Facilities include two tea shops (one of them vegetarian), a post office/shop, toilets and a telephone.

UPPER ARLEY

To the Saxons Arley was Ernley - "the clearing where eagles live" - though it's likely the eagles were buzzards, which may still be seen today. The footbridge, built in 1971, replaces a ferry service which was first recorded in 1323; the slipway from which the ferry operated still survives. The village street is lined with a variety of interesting buildings, culminating in 12th-century St Peter's Church, which contains among its memorials a 13th-century tomb, believed to be that of the unfortunate Sir Walter de Balun, a would-be crusader who never reached the Holy Land because he was killed in a tournament celebrating his marriage.

Leaving Upper Arley, walk south on the east bank, on a surfaced pathway at first, before continuing across wooded slopes above the river. The path is shared by the Severn Way and the Worcestershire Way, an 80km/50 mile regional route. At Worrall's Grove the path forks. Branch left and cross a footbridge, then turn right immediately, leaving the Worcestershire Way. A few strides further on ascend left, then descend right, on a wide track through Eymore Wood ❶. This is the easternmost extension of Wyre Forest, and although part of it has been turned into a plantation, most of the trees are the attractive European larch, which turns gold in autumn.

When the track forks, stay by the river to pass under Victoria Bridge ❷, cast at Coalbrookdale and designed by John Fowler, the engineer responsible for the original London Underground. The bridge featured in the 1978 remake of John Buchan's 'The Thirty-nine Steps', starring Robert Powell.

Further on, the path leaves Eymore Wood to round Trimpley Reservoirs ❸, constructed in the 1960s to supplement the Elan Valley water supply to Birmingham.

Beyond the reservoirs, the way continues along the edge of woodland, to become a broad stony track at a car park adjoining the Elan Aqueduct ❹. Continue beyond the car park onto a surfaced lane.

Follow the lane, taking care against approaching traffic, until, just after a house named Bridewell, you turn right, over a stile, around a field edge, and so set off across a number of riverside meadows. A broad track leads past the abutments of a dismantled viaduct, beyond which a path heads into a park.

BEWDLEY

When the path bends left, continue beside the river until the route is deflected around the rowing club to a lane leading to Wribbenhall and the bridge into Bewdley, a little town with a full range of facilities. The Tourist Information Centre ❺ is on Load Street. In addition, Wyre Forest Visitor Centre ❻ and West Midland Safari Park ❼ are both nearby.

At the bridge, either cross the road or use the underpass and proceed into Stourport Road. Leave the road when it bends left, and cross a forecourt on the right. Keep on along a wide riverside path. When this forks stay by the river and press on towards Bewdley bypass and Blackstone Rock.

Severn Valley Railway

The River Severn passing through Bewdley

THE place we now know as Bewdley was given to the Norman baron Roger de Mortimer soon after the Conquest and its name is probably derived from the French beau lieu - "beautiful place" - a description which still holds good today. It has been a trading centre since prehistoric times when it lay on the route of a Bronze Age track now known as the Clee-Clun Ridgeway. However, it was the Severn that made Bewdley's fortune as the developing town made full use of its riverside position to engage in trade, gradually becoming a major inland port. Documentary evidence shows that trade was well established by 1412, and the building of Bewdley's first bridge in 1447 gave further impetus to development. Borough status was achieved in 1472 with the granting of a charter by Edward IV.

Bewdley's position at a river crossing in the Welsh Marches gave it a certain strategic significance too, especially as it was in the hands of the Mortimers, most powerful of the Marcher lords. For a time, Bewdley appears to have been the administrative centre of the Council in the Marches of Wales before this moved to Ludlow. Just out of town is Tickenhill Manor, which was often visited by royalty and was the venue for Prince Arthur's marriage to Katherine of Aragon in 1499.

But Bewdley was about trade, not politics. It became one of the four principal ports on the river, along with Worcester, Gloucester and Bridgnorth. Goods coming upstream from Bristol were loaded onto pack-ponies and wagons to be distributed throughout the Midlands, and Bewdley's own trade goods, mainly brass, horn and leather products, met with a ready market downstream. Tradition has it that the Bewdley boatmen would not allow carriage of goods upstream except in their own craft, a practice that resulted in Bristol and Gloucester petitioning Parliament in protest.

Bewdley's early prosperity is reflected in the splendid buildings lining the narrow, winding streets and the long, straight waterfront, the finest in the Midlands. Many of the houses are medieval timber-framed structures, which were given new brick façades in the 18th century, making Bewdley a Georgian town superimposed on a medieval street plan.

Economic decline set in when Bewdley reputedly refused the "stinking ditch" - the Staffordshire and Worcestershire Canal - which was, therefore, joined to the Severn further south, giving rise to a new, and soon prosperous, town - Stourport. Bewdley slid into decay and obscurity as the Industrial Revolution passed it by. The subsequent lack of funds kept development to a minimum, thus preserving the old town which is such a pleasure to explore today.

Many visitors don't venture beyond the waterfront and the shops, but there is so much more to see, with a fresh surprise around every corner. Load Street, the main thoroughfare, with St Anne's Church at one end, Telford's graceful bridge at the other, has a pleasing blend of architectural styles, though it is predominantly Georgian. It offers shops, pubs, cafés, a Tourist Information Centre and what is probably one of the best local museums in the country.

High Street, where you would normally expect to find shops, is almost entirely residential, reflecting the way the commercial focus shifted as the river trade grew in importance. It's easily missed, but well worth seeking out because it has some fine buildings. Its continuation is called Lower Park, and number 15 was the birthplace in 1867 of Stanley Baldwin, Prime Minister during the abdication crisis in the 1930s. On his resignation in 1937 he was created Earl Baldwin of Bewdley.

The waterfront (Severnside North and South) is lined with gracious houses and some former warehouses now converted into apartments. On the east bank of the river is Wribbenhall, which has impressive former quays, 17th- and 18th-century buildings and some fascinating little streets and alleyways. It's also where you'll find the beautifully restored Bewdley Station, headquarters of the Severn Valley Railway.

Bewdley could hardly be more fortunate in its setting: as if the presence of the river were not enough, it also lies on the edge of Wyre Forest, one of Britain's largest areas of ancient semi-natural woodland. Though much of it has been planted with conifers, there is still extensive broad-leaved woodland, rich in wildlife and designated a National Nature Reserve. You can reach the forest by a short walk upstream on the west bank of the river to Dowles Brook, where you turn left. Or hop on a Ludlow-bound bus and get off at the Visitor Centre.

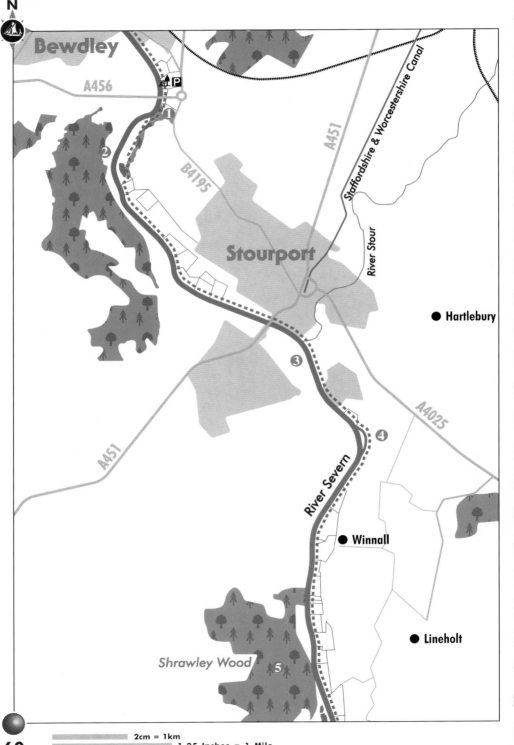

N

Bewdley

A456

P

2

B4195

Stourport

Staffordshire & Worcestershire Canal

A451

River Stour

● Hartlebury

3

A4025

4

A451

River Severn

● Winnall

● Lineholt

Shrawley Wood

5

2cm = 1km
1.25 Inches = 1 Mile

BLACKSTONE ROCK

Continue under the Bewdley bypass and onto an enclosed path, leaving it at a bend to turn right over a stile into a riverside field and on below Blackstone Rock **1**, riddled with caves which once provided dwellings for hermits. There was a ford at Blackstone and it is believed that the caves may also have provided shelter for travellers prevented by high water from crossing to Bewdley in the days before the town's first bridge was built.

Having passed Blackstone Rock keep forward to a stile beside a gate. Climb briefly through a rock cutting to reach a large arable field, shortly forking left along the left edge of the field, below sandstone cliffs.

On the far bank you can see Ribbesford House **2**, its Tudor framework hidden beneath a later façade. During World War II officers of the Free French Forces under General de Gaulle were based here for a time.

Not far into the field you can cut into adjoining woodland at a stile, and continue at the woodland edge to a grassy path through bracken. Pass a pond and cross a field to a stile giving access to the riverbank and walk along the edge of a caravan site. A stile on the far side gives onto a narrow path running above the river.

As you approach Lickhill Manor, stay beside the river to pass Stourport Motor Yacht and Bungalow Association, then continue through parkland as you approach Stourport. Keep on under Stourport Bridge (A451).

STOURPORT-ON-SEVERN

Stourport owes its existence to the Staffordshire and Worcestershire Canal, opened in 1772. It was originally intended that it should join the Severn at Bewdley but when that idea was rejected, a hamlet called Lower Mitton was chosen instead. This acquired the new name of Stourport and rapidly prospered, soon outstripping Bewdley. Stourport is the only British town to come into being solely as a result of the canal system. The canal basins remain busy today, with boat repair yards and many day-trippers and leisure users. No longer an inland port so much as an inland resort, Stourport still retains some of its Georgian elegance. The imposing Tontine Inn makes a good backdrop for the locks, which mark the junction of canal and river, while towpaths and bridges enable you to explore the colourful wharves and basins.

Beyond the bridge, go forward towards an amusement park entrance and then bear right to go through Stourport Basins. Pass the Tontine Hotel and the Angel Inn before crossing the River Stour at its confluence with the Severn. Notice Redstone Rock **3** towering over the other bank, once inhabited by cave-dwelling hermits who probably also manned the ferry at Redstone Crossing, first recorded in the 13th century.

Pass through a boatyard, and onto a narrow path that leads to a large industrial warehouse. Keep to the right of this and go past Lincomb Lock **4**, the northernmost one on the river. Beyond it you revert to a grassy path through undergrowth, which takes you on to a footbridge, and into light woodland before reaching the edge of an enclosed area near a caravan park.

The route continues along the top of an embankment. Go forward and cross a slipway, and on the other side cross a grassed playing area to rejoin the riverside path. Just as you come to the end of the path, turn left over a stile to a footbridge. Immediately turn right to return to a grassy path along the top of the riverbank opposite Shrawley Wood **5**, notable for its abundance of small-leaved lime, a species that is nationally rare but locally common. Shrawley is one of the finest limewoods in Britain.

Water crowfoot near Blackstone Rock

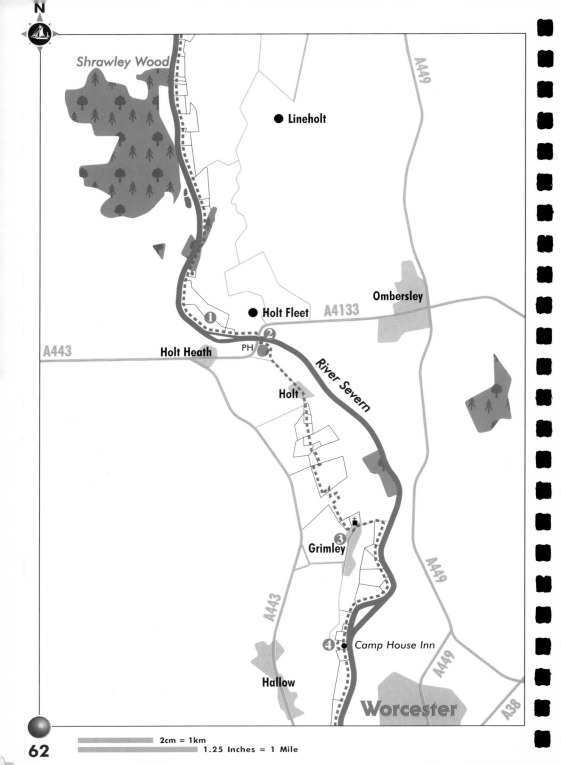

N

Shrawley Wood

Lineholt

A449

Ombersley

Holt Fleet

A4133

A443

Holt Heath

PH

River Severn

Holt

Grimley

A443

A449

Camp House Inn

A449

Hallow

Worcester

A38

2cm = 1km
1.25 Inches = 1 Mile

From Shrawley Wood to Holt Fleet the Way closely follows the river, and near Mutton Hall joins a woodchip track before passing through a caravan park into a large pasture. Go around its edge, following the river, and soon passing Holt Lock ❶.

At Holt Fleet, where facilities include a small supermarket, a telephone, two pubs and a café, the route crosses the river. Head towards the bridge, then turn left just past a cottage and climb steps to the road (A4133).

Cross the bridge ❷, designed by Telford in 1828, and turn down to the left of the Holt Fleet pub. Cross the rear car park, bearing right to a stile. Go up steps into woodland then over a stile to emerge in a sloping pasture. Go forward, climbing to cross a stile and meet a concrete path. Turn left to follow it through Holt.

HOLT

A castle and church face each other across the lane, providing something of an architectural feast. The castle's origins lie in the 11th century, but the earliest part of the present structure is the 14th-century tower built by John Beauchamp. St Martin's Church dates from c1080 and is one of the finest Norman churches in the county, with superb carvings on the exterior walls and much of interest inside. An unexpected link with an earlier section of the Severn Way is the 9th-centenary oak in the churchyard, planted in 1980 and grown from an acorn taken from the Gospel Oak at Cressage.

At Holt Grange go forward across a cattle grid onto a broad track, which continues to Top Barn Farm, where you go through the complex of buildings and forward down a track. At a junction turn right and, 30m/yds later, left on a broad track. Just after meeting a surfaced lane, go over a stile on the left, and along the edge of woodland.

As you draw level with a pond on the left, turn right over a footbridge, and then, at the edge of quarry workings, turn left to another footbridge. Cross this and turn right, aiming for Grimley Church. When you emerge onto a stony track, turn right, following signs for Church Farm.

At overhead powerlines, turn left on a grassy track parallel with the lines, and then climb to a stile at a powerline junction. Beyond this keep to the field margin, and, on the far side of the field, go left towards Grimley Church ❸.

At a gate, turn right to go through the churchyard, passing in front of the main door, and continuing between headstones to a road. St Bartholomew's is of 12th-century origin but was rebuilt in the 19th century. The explorer Sir Samuel Baker (1821-93) is buried in the churchyard.

Turn left, passing the Wagonwheel Inn and following the road round onto a track leading to the Severn. Turn right over a footbridge to rejoin the river. The delightful path soon leads past Bevere Island and the adjacent lock.

BEVERE

Bevere Island, often known as the Camp, formed a useful refuge for Worcester's citizens in the past - from Danish raiders, from civil war and from the plague which, ironically, was probably brought upriver by the trowmen. Bevere Lock, formerly Camp Lock, was completed in 1844.

Keep going to Camp House Inn ❹, licensed by Cromwell after the Battle of Worcester. As you reach the pub, turn right, then left through a caravan site to rejoin the riverbank.

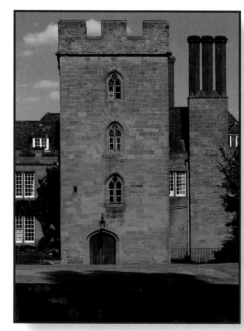

Holt Castle

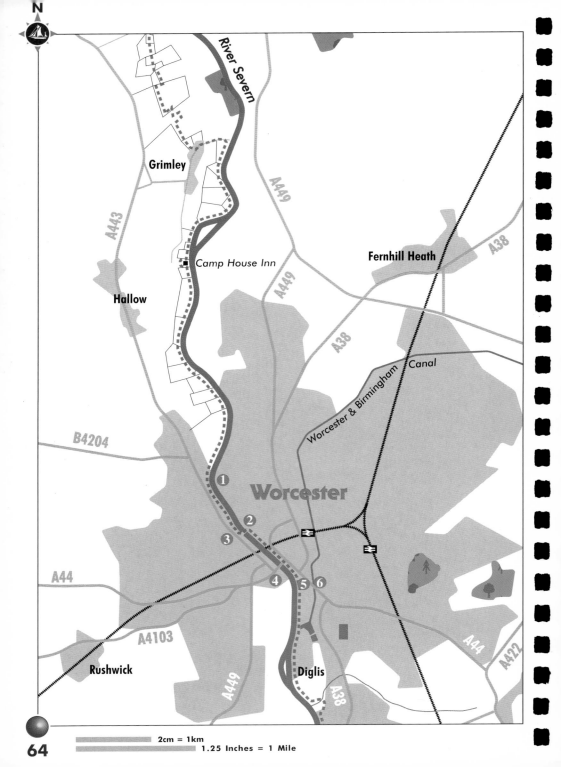

N

River Severn

A449

A38

Grimley

A443

Camp House Inn

Fernhill Heath

A449

A38

Hallow

Worcester & Birmingham Canal

B4204

①
Worcester

②

③

A44

④
⑤ ⑥

A4103

Rushwick

Diglis

A449

A38

A44

A422

64

2cm = 1km

1.25 Inches = 1 Mile

Between Camp House Inn and Worcester the Severn Way never leaves the river's company, and for some distance passes through woodland that effectively screens the buildings of Worcester from view. Gradually, however, the city begins to make its presence felt as Barbourne is glimpsed on the far bank. Kepax Ferry used to operate here, close to the present-day waterworks ❶.

THE DOG AND DUCK

Before long you reach the site of another extinct ferry, the Dog and Duck, named after a pub which later became the ferryman's home. There was a wharf here, serving Martley, Clifton and other points west. At the top of the steep bank is King Stephen's Mount, the site of a fortification built in the 12th-century civil war of Stephen and Matilda. Ferry Steps ascend to the road here but the Way keeps to the riverbank.

It is a common and pleasant sight along this stretch to see rowing boats of various sizes sculling up and down the river from their base near Worcester Racecourse, while narrowboats and cruisers from further afield are also frequently seen. The Racecourse is contained within Pitchcroft ❷, a huge tree-bordered common, where horse racing began in the 18th century.

The surfaced path leads on to reach Sabrina Bridge ❸, a stylish cycle/footbridge opened in 1992 and given the Roman name for the Severn. Cross the bridge and continue downstream, walking beneath the ornate railway bridge over which trains pass on the scenic journey to the Malverns and Hereford. Keep on, passing toilets, a snack bar and the pleasure steamers berthed by North Quay. A spur from the railway once ran along here. It was hoped to extend it to Diglis, but the Cathedral authorities objected and so it terminated at South Quay.

Near Worcester Bridge ❹, built by John Gwynn in 1781, cross the road at a pedestrian crossing. Having crossed, turn right to a busy junction, and cross with care, going forward into South Quay, where former warehouses have been converted into apartments and a restaurant. Up to 100 swans can usually be seen below the quay or nearby. On the opposite bank, screened by trees, is the county cricket ground, New Road. Continue alongside the medieval city walls, past the Old Palace and the Cathedral ❺, staying beside the river to reach Diglis, where the Worcester and Birmingham Canal joins the Severn and where there are locks and a weir across the river.

DIGLIS (WORCESTER)

The canal opened in 1815 and links Diglis directly with Gas Street Basin in Birmingham, the heart of Britain's canal system. Trade built up steadily, and was boosted after the construction of the Gloucester and Sharpness Ship Canal, but the opening of the Birmingham and Gloucester Railway in 1841 led to a reduction in canal traffic and from then on it was a case of steady decline, though it was not until 1961 that the last commercial cargo, of chocolate crumb, left Diglis for Cadbury's factory at Bournville. Nowadays the canal is enormously popular with leisure users, and is an important link in the inland waterways network. It's well worth exploring Diglis Basins, always busy with both narrowboats and sea-going vessels. The canal towpath provides a pleasant route into town, passing directly by the Commandery Civil War Centre ❻ and close by the Cathedral. You'll find the Tourist Information Centre at the Guildhall on High Street.

Easy access along the Severn Way in Worcester

Worcester Cathedral

FOR over 2,000 years there has been a settlement at Worcester, as numerous Iron Age indicate. It first attained a degree of prominence in the Roman period, when a flourishing iron smelting industry developed and a port was established, mainly for transporting salt from the mines at Droitwich. After the Romans left, the Saxons moved in and Worcester became an ecclesiastical and political centre in West Mercia, the kingdom of the Hwicce people. It was under the Normans, however, that Worcester began to grow into a city of considerable importance. They built a castle and a new cathedral and the city received its first Royal Charter from Richard the Lionheart in 1189.

Throughout the following centuries, Worcester grew and prospered, making good use of the Severn for fishing and trade. Politically, life was relatively uneventful, except during the two civil wars of 1135-48 and 1642-51. In the latter, both the first skirmish and the final battle took place close to the city, and Worcester's staunch loyalty to the Stuart cause earned it the name of the Faithful City from a grateful Charles II. Economically, it was doing well too - a census in 1661 listed it as the eleventh city of the kingdom. It continued to thrive, with rapid expansion in the Georgian and Victorian periods, but the 20th century brought decline, partly because rail and road had superseded canal and river transport.

Over the last two decades, however, the city has expanded again, with large areas of former countryside now given over to housing. As this is mostly to the north and east it doesn't impinge on the river, and walkers on the Severn Way are likely to be agreeably surprised at how painless is the transition from countryside to city. Stay on the Severn Way and you could pass through urban Worcester in minutes, hardly conscious of it as a city at all, except for the traffic on the road bridge, and, by way of contrast, the sublime view of the Cathedral beyond. But it would be a great shame to pass by without exploring Worcester, for much evidence of its rich and varied past remains visible.

Only a few suggestions can be made here, so the Tourist Information Centre is an obvious starting point, and is itself housed in one of Worcester's main assets - the splendid Guildhall of 1721-23. Though it's a flamboyant building, a close look will reveal entertaining details that often go unnoticed; such as the devil's head, believed to represent Oliver Cromwell, nailed by the ears above the doorway.

The city's main glory is the Cathedral, with its superb Severnside location. A wooden cathedral is known to have existed in 680 but in 1084 Bishop Wulstan began to build in stone, and parts of his cathedral still survive. Further building and alteration took place between 1225 and 1395, by when the present building was more or less complete, though there has been much restoration since. The Cathedral is packed with interest but the main features include King John's Tomb, Prince Arthur's Chantry, St Wulstan's Crypt and the 14th-century misericords, often described as the finest in England.

Numerous buildings of great interest surround the Cathedral. Don't miss the 14th-century Edgar Tower, the Kings' School buildings in College Green, the Deanery, the Watergate, the Old Palace or the ruins of the Guesten Hall. All of these are easily accessible from the Severn Way. Not far away, on Sidbury, is the Commandery, originally a hospital founded by Wulstan, though the present building dates from the 15th century. It served as Charles II's headquarters for a time and now functions as an excellent museum devoted to the Civil War.

In fact, Worcester has a number of good museums, with the City Museum and Art Gallery on Foregate Street hosting a permanent display about the River Severn. The picturesque Museum of Local Life on Friar Street is the favourite for many people, and Friar Street is itself one of the most attractive in the city, with many timber-framed buildings, including the National Trust's Greyfriars. Adjoining New Street and Cornmarket are worth seeing too.

Royal Worcester porcelain is famous throughout the world and the factory is by the river between the Cathedral and Diglis. The associated museum houses the world's finest collection of Royal Worcester.

Another big name is Worcester Sauce, and the Lea and Perrins factory stands on Midland Road, which is not far from Fort Royal Park, reached by a short walk up London Road from the Commandery and well worth the climb for the magnificent view of the Cathedral, still effortlessly dominating the modern city, despite the inevitable abundance of intrusive new buildings.

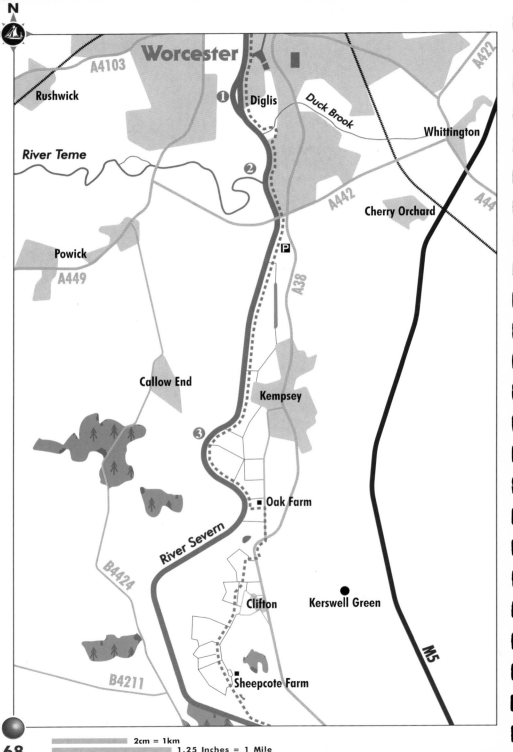

N

Worcester

A4103

A422

Rushwick

① Diglis

Duck Brook

Whittington

River Teme

②

A442

A44

Cherry Orchard

Powick

A449

P

A38

Callow End

Kempsey

③

Oak Farm

River Severn

B4424

Clifton

Kerswell Green

B4211

Sheepcote Farm

M5

2cm = 1km

1.25 Inches = 1 Mile

Worcester marks a change in the Severn, which is now much wider and flows through gentler countryside. Although much of the route between Worcester and the hamlet of Clifton faithfully follows the river, there are places where deviations are necessary.

From Diglis Locks ❶, go forward onto a riverside path once more, until deflected away from the river by in-flowing Duck Brook. Cross the brook at a footbridge, turning right through woodland to rejoin the riverbank. To your left is the suburb of St Peter's, while across the river, just north of its confluence with the Teme ❷, is one of the sites on which the Battle of Worcester was fought in 1651.

BATTLE OF WORCESTER

The English Civil War began in 1642 with a Royalist victory in a brief skirmish at nearby Powick Bridge on the River Teme. In 1651, the final battle of the war was fought by the riverside here, and at other sites in and around the city. Victory went to Cromwell and Charles Stuart was forced into exile until recalled to the throne in 1660.

The riverside path eventually enters Ketch Caravan Park. Proceed along an embankment to the far side and pass under the A422 onto a track. This becomes a woodland path and later goes through the grounds of the Severn Motor Yacht Club before reaching a large open field, Upper Ham, and then another caravan park. Continuing along a broad green track, go past the Seaborne Yacht Company, across a slipway and past more caravans at Kempsey.

KEMPSEY

This is one of the county's oldest villages, the site of both Iron Age and Roman settlements. St Mary's Church overlooks the Severn Way and is unexpectedly grand in scale, with a notable Early English chancel of 1250-60. The manor was owned by the Bishops of Worcester throughout the Middle Ages and they had a palace near the church. There are shops, pubs and a telephone in the village.

Proceed through Lower Ham, passing the former Pixham ferry crossing ❸, where Simon de Montfort, in revolt against Henry III, crossed the Severn on his way to defeat and death at the Battle of Evesham in 1265. The ferry ceased operation in 1939.

On the far side of Lower Ham, at a stile, descend right to a riverbank path. Eventually steps bring you up from the river into an arable field. Cross to Oak Farm then turn right along Old Road. Walk to a junction and turn right beside the A38, crossing to a footway on the other side. Follow the road round a bend until, about 300m/yds after joining it, you can leave it on the right, at a gate.

Walk alongside a hedge until it ends, then turn left across an arable field. On the far side climb a stile beside a gate, and go half-right across the next field. After another stile, turn left, aiming to the right of the buildings at Clifton Lower Farm. As you pass them, go left through a gate to join a farm track, turning right to a stile at the edge of an open field.

Go forward along its left-hand edge, and cross a stile in a field corner. Proceed along the edges of a couple of fields to meet a track at Sheepcote Farm. Turn right, following the track round a field edge until you can leave it at a stile on the right. Then turn left across an arable field and over a stile to rejoin the riverbank.

Cowslip flowering

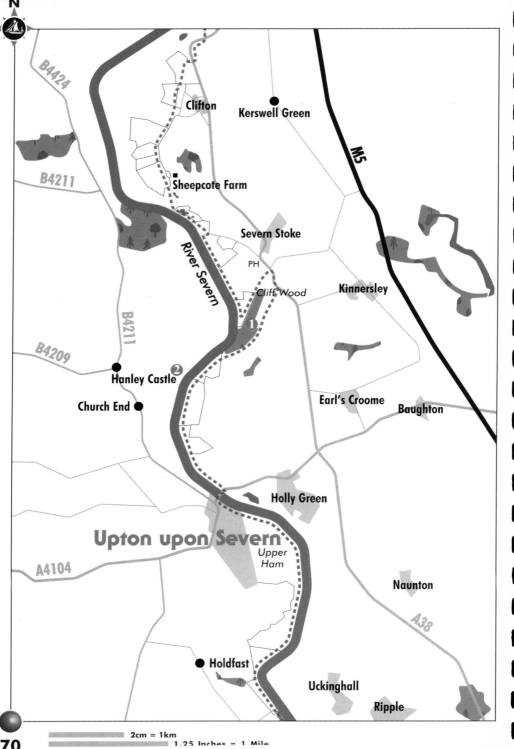

N

B4424

Clifton

Kerswell Green

M5

B4211

Sheepcote Farm

River Severn

Severn Stoke

PH

Cliff Wood

Kinnersley

1

B4211

B4209

2

Hanley Castle

Church End

Earl's Croome

Baughton

Holly Green

Upton upon Severn

Upper Ham

A4104

Naunton

A38

Holdfast

Uckinghall

Ripple

2cm = 1km

1.25 Inches = 1 Mile

Except for a couple of deviations, the Severn Way flirts closely with the river throughout this section. Upton upon Severn is an ideal place for a break, with abundant pubs, shops, cafés and restaurants.

Having rejoined the riverbank just beyond Sheepcote Farm, you soon leave it, albeit briefly, to cross a stile in a fence, and bear right across an arable field. Meeting a lane on the far side, turn right and rejoin the riverbank.

Eventually, further riverside progress is barred by Cliff Wood, above which rises Severn Bank ❶, an imposing 19th-century mansion, with Gothic windows and crenellated walls.

The route turns left along a field edge to meet the A38 at Severn Stoke. The Severn Way turns right, but a short detour to the left will take you to the village, with its three pubs and interesting Norman church, dedicated to St Denys.

The Severn Way, after a couple of bends, turns right again onto a lane, going past the entrance to Severn Bank and onto a driveway to the Coach House. Just as you approach the latter, bear left through a gate onto a grassy track that descends past Cliff Wood to rejoin riverside pastures.

On the far bank now, set against the backdrop of the Malvern Hills, is timber-framed Severn End ❷, the home of the Lechmere family for 700 years, though the present house was built in the 17th century and restored in 1896.

Also on the far bank, a little further south, is Hanley Castle, which once had a busy quay by the river for the export of local pottery. The eponymous castle was built for King John in 1205 but only earthworks remain today.

On the final approach to Upton, having crossed Fish Meadow, the route is channelled through an underpass. On the other side turn right to climb to the road, and then cross Upton Bridge.

UPTON UPON SEVERN

Upton's economic fortunes have always depended on its position by the Severn. As early as 1289, the Bishop of Hereford was landing his wine supplies from Bristol here and Upton was in the process of becoming a thriving port. Its zenith came in the 18th century when timber, coal, salt, cider and bricks were among the main commodities traded.

When the river trade declined Upton fell back on fishing and farming, which provided a measure of prosperity, yet not enough to sustain much development, so that, like Bewdley, it remains relatively unspoilt. Today, trade comes mainly by road, but it still depends on the river, for tourism now plays a significant part in the local economy.

Upton is a lovely little town that makes the most of its riverside setting and stages several festivals throughout the year, with many of the main events taking place in Fish Meadow. Other attractions include a colourful marina, pleasure boat trips, Civil War associations and a feast of beautiful period buildings, most prominent of which is the "Pepperpot" - the cupola-topped tower of an otherwise demolished medieval church. The splendid White Lion, a former coaching inn, was the main setting for Henry Fielding's novel 'Tom Jones'. The Tourist Information Centre is on High Street.

Having crossed the bridge into Upton, turn sharply left onto Waterside, passing pubs and elegant Georgian houses before entering Upper Ham, which includes Upton Meadow, a nature reserve belonging to Plantlife. After leaving the Ham, the delightful riverside path continues southwards.

The Pepperpot, Upton upon Severn

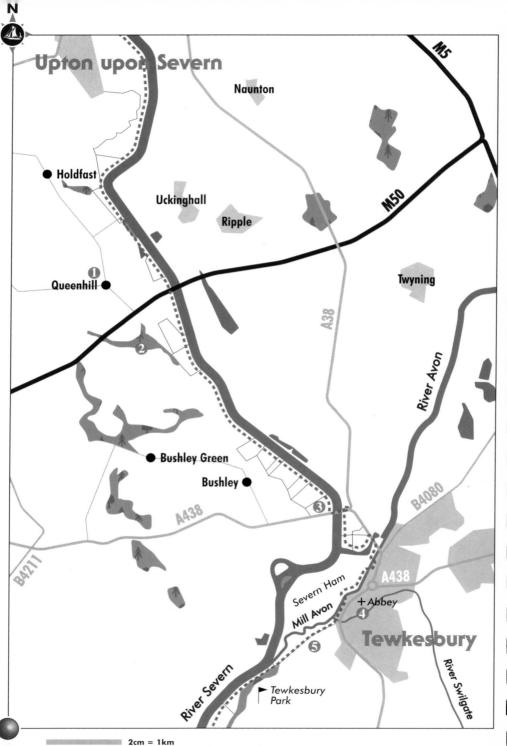

Upton upon Severn

Naunton

M5

Holdfast

Uckinghall

Ripple

M50

A38

Twyning

Queenhill ①

②

River Avon

Bushley Green ●

Bushley ●

③

A438

B4080

B4211

Severn Ham

Mill Avon

A438

+Abbey ④

Tewkesbury

River Severn

⑤

River Swilgate

► Tewkesbury
Park

2cm = 1km
1.25 Inches = 1 Mile

Easy walking lies between Holdfast and the outskirts of Tewkesbury, as the route continues pleasantly along the true right bank of the river. Only the sound of the M50 disturbs the peace, and that only briefly.

HOLDFAST

Holdfast is a scattered settlement with no real centre, and makes little impression on the riverside walker. In the past, the local economy was based on both fishing and farming and in the early 20th century Holdfast was famous for sweet peas, grown by Hilda Hemus on a farm called Paradise. They were sent to the London markets on the train from Upton and attracted such renown that Edward VII asked that Hilda should be presented to him at court.

Just south of Holdfast is Queenhill ❶, where Sir Edward Elgar is said to have found inspiration while admiring the view from the church porch. He might feel less inspired if he could return today, now that the M50 passes within 150m/yds of the church.

Having passed under the motorway you will notice an imposing mansion to the right. Previously known as Pull Court, this was for centuries the home of the Dowdeswell family, but is now Bredon School ❷, a boys' boarding school.

Not far south of the school, the Severn forms the county boundary, with the far bank now in Gloucestershire. As you approach Tewkesbury, a wooded cliff towers above the other bank. Topped with the earthworks of a motte and bailey castle, this is known as Mythe Tute, and has associations with King John.

Just beyond this you meet Mythe Bridge ❸, a handsome single span of iron completed by Telford in 1826. Turn right over a stile and shortly go left to join the A438. Cross the bridge, going forward to a footpath on the left. Turn down steps through two iron gates, and then turn left towards the river until you can pass beneath Mythe Bridge.

Follow a constructed pathway past Severn Trent's waterworks, and then a field-edge path to the confluence of the Severn and the Old Avon, one of two channels into which the River Avon splits. Meeting the road at Beaufort Bridge, turn right to King John's Bridge, and then right again onto a towpath alongside the Mill Avon. When you reach a flour mill turn left across a bridge and then right to a nearby footbridge.

TEWKESBURY

Few walkers would wish to follow the Severn Way through Tewkesbury without exploring the town centre. There is a lot to see, including a magnificent abbey, and abundant facilities of all kinds. You'll find the Tourist Information Centre on Barton Street.

Over the footbridge, turn left along the edge of Severn Ham. Recross the Mill Avon at the next footbridge, at Abbey Mill. Walk up Mill Street to meet the A38 near the abbey ❹ and turn right. Just after the road crosses the River Swilgate (a tributary of the Mill Avon) turn right into Lower Lode Lane, which leads to an ancient ford.

A short way along the lane is a signpost for Bloody Meadow ❺, the site of the Battle of Tewkesbury in 1471, when the Yorkists won a significant victory over the Lancastrians in one of the most decisive battles of the Wars of the Roses. At the end of the lane, you rejoin the river by the Cheltenham College Boathouse. Go past this and through a metal gate to resume riverside walking.

The banded demoiselle is a common sight along the Severn

Tewkesbury Abbey

THOUGH only a small town, Tewkesbury has over 200 Listed Buildings in the centre alone, and every one of them is worth looking at. Add to that its riverside setting, its glorious abbey and some notable historical connections too, and you have what is undoubtedly one of the most charming and fascinating towns in the country.

There is evidence of Roman occupation at Tewkesbury and the Saxons certainly had a settlement there, but it was only when the Normans arrived that the great abbey was founded, and for the next three centuries Tewkesbury benefited from the patronage of such influential families as FitzHamon, de Clare, Despenser, Beauchamp and Neville, as well as enjoying strong Royal connections. The Battle of Tewkesbury in 1471 was a major event in national history, bringing to an end the second phase of the Wars of the Roses, and re-establishing Edward IV on the throne.

Tewkesbury prospered as a market town and trading centre, largely due to the river traffic. It was an industrial town too, important for both cloth and clothing, as well as milling, malting and brewing. By the early 19th century it had also become a popular staging post, with about 30 stagecoaches a day passing through, as Charles Dickens well knew when he had Mr Pickwick stop off at the Hop Pole Hotel. But, bypassed by the railway, which was routed through nearby Ashchurch, Tewkesbury slipped into stagnation after 1850. In more recent years light industry has become established and the M5 has helped to make the town into a distribution centre. Once again Tewkesbury is thriving. A popular residential and shopping centre, it has a flourishing tourist trade too, thanks to those years of stagnation which ensured the preservation of the old townscape. It also stands at the southernmost point of the Midlands' inland waterways network, making it a natural magnet for the boating fraternity.

As with other Severnside towns, the river has had a major influence on Tewkesbury's fortunes. It stands at the confluence of the Severn and Avon, which are joined by tributaries such as the River Swilgate, Tirle Brook and Carrant Brook. Inevitably, therefore, Tewkesbury has always been vulnerable to flooding and has had to limit its spread accordingly. Industrial growth has been concentrated at Northway and Ashchurch, leaving the old town relatively untouched, with the medieval street pattern still much in evidence. Church Street, High Street and Barton Street are graced by one of the finest collections of timber-framed and brick buildings in existence, many of them dating from the 15th, 16th and 17th centuries. Another remarkable feature is the number of narrow alleyways leading off the main streets, though only about 30 remain of the original 90 or so. Most date from the 17th and 18th centuries when increased pressure for housing led to the practice of infilling on narrow plots behind the street frontages. Nearly all of these old alleys and courts are worth exploring, though the most famous is Old Baptist Chapel Court which leads to what is probably southern England's first Baptist chapel, converted from existing buildings in 1623.

Tewkesbury's finest building is, of course, the Abbey Church of St Mary, which is magnificent from almost any angle, but especially when viewed from the south across the River Swilgate. The west front and the massive tower, the largest and finest in Britain, are particularly powerful. The Abbey has the size and appearance of a cathedral but it was a monastic church and is now the parish church, the townsfolk having bought it from Henry VIII for £453 in 1540 at the Dissolution of the Monasteries. It was built by Robert FitzHamon who brought much of the stone from Caen in his native Normandy, transporting it by sea and then up the Severn. Tewkesbury Abbey became one of the most powerful in the kingdom and was the last of the monasteries to be dissolved by Henry VIII. Inside, one of the most striking features is the set of 14 Norman pillars supporting the roof and there is a collection of tombs and monuments which is second in both quality and quantity only to Westminster Abbey.

Tewkesbury's waterfront is interesting too. At one time there were several mills on the Mill Avon, which was probably cut by the monks in the 12th century to power the abbey mill. A later Abbey Mill still survives on the site of the original building but is now a restuarant. Healing's Mill is still working; it was built in 1865 and it produces flour from grain carried from Sharpness Docks by 'Tirley' and 'Chaceley', the last two working barges on the Severn.

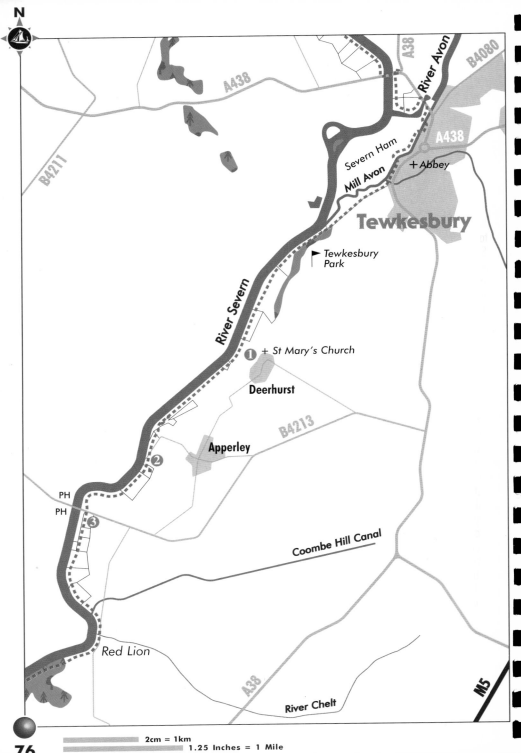

N

River Avon

A38

B4080

A438

A438

B4211

Severn Ham

Mill Avon

+ Abbey

Tewkesbury

► Tewkesbury Park

River Severn

❶ + St Mary's Church

Deerhurst

B4213

Apperley

PH

❷

PH

❸

Coombe Hill Canal

Red Lion

A38

M5

River Chelt

2cm = 1km

1.25 Inches = 1 Mile

Between Tewkesbury and the outskirts of Gloucester, the Severn Way barely leaves the river, spending its time on verdant bankside paths or in adjacent pastures. There is little scope for losing one's way, and only a few route directions are necessary to bring you to the edge of Gloucester.

Moving on from the outskirts of Tewkesbury, the route soon passes the remarkable village of Deerhurst, a short diversion into which is highly recommended - just turn left by an isolated oak tree.

DEERHURST

The village is unique in possessing two outstanding Anglo-Saxon buildings: Odda's Chapel and St Mary's Church. Stone-built Odda's Chapel ❶ is a rare example of an almost complete Saxon building. It was built in 1056 but a timber-framed farmhouse, Abbot's Court, was attached to it in the 16th century and for many years the chapel, its origins forgotten, served as the farmhouse kitchen. Its true identity was discovered during repairs to the house in 1885.

The Priory Church of St Mary is even older. It is known that a monastery existed on the site in 804 and the present nave is probably the monastic church, built in the late 8th or early 9th century. However, parts of St Mary's are thought to date from the 7th century, while much of the rest belongs to the 10th century, though there is also later work. The double-headed triangular window in the nave is one of the most remarkable features, renowned for both its rarity and its quality.

The priory was, for a time, the leading religious foundation in the region, and it was here, in 1016, that King Edmund Ironside met King Cnut of Denmark to sign a treaty defining the boundary between Saxon England and the Danelaw.

Other foundations at Evesham, Gloucester, Winchcombe and Tewkesbury soon eclipsed the priory, and it became a cell of Tewkesbury Abbey. The priory church became the parish church after the Dissolution of the Monasteries.

Returning to the Severn Way, keep on along the riverside embankment to reach the Coal House Inn ❷ on a former coal wharf serving Apperley and nearby villages. Go forward towards a caravan park and, beyond this, enter a large open field, remaining with the river as it curves round to Haw Bridge ❸. The route does not cross the bridge, but on the other side of the river are two pubs and a campsite. The bridge was built in 1961, after a tanker barge demolished its predecessor, built in 1825 to replace Haw Passage Ferry.

Cross the B4213 and go down to Bridge House. A short way on, go left over a stile into a field and turn right along the edge of riverside meadows that eventually lead to the junction of Coombe Hill Canal with the River Severn.

COOMBE HILL CANAL

The canal was built in 1796-97 to carry coal from the Forest of Dean to Cheltenham. It got only as far as Coombe Hill Wharf, beside the present A38, where goods were transferred to wagons. It was never a successful venture because of constant problems with flooding. Competition, first in the form of a tramway from Gloucester Docks, followed by the railway, led to its final abandonment in 1876 and it is now a Gloucestershire Wildlife Trust nature reserve, rich in plant and animal life.

Keep going to join a road at Fletcher's Leap, where the River Chelt flows into the Severn. Turn right to reach the Red Lion at Wainlode.

Odda's Chapel

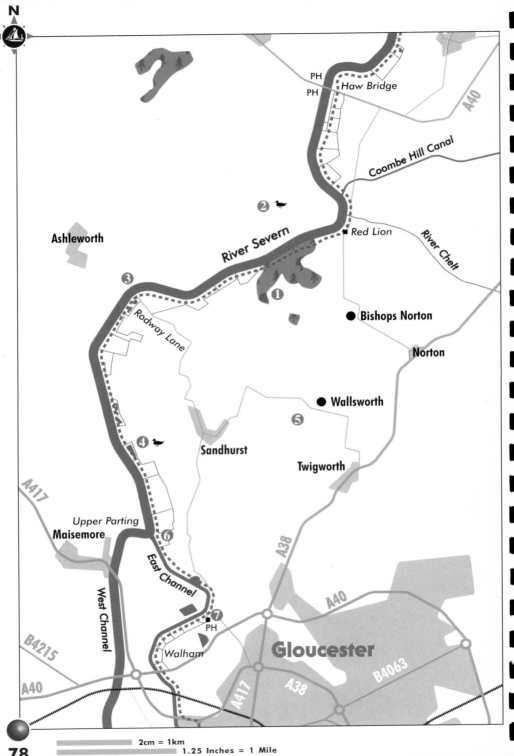

N

PH
PH
Haw Bridge

Coombe Hill Canal

②

River Severn

Ashleworth

River Chelt

Red Lion

③

Rodway Lane

①

● Bishops Norton

Norton

● Wallsworth

⑤

④

Sandhurst

Twigworth

A417

Upper Parting

Maisemore

⑥

East Channel

West Channel

A38

A40

A417

A40

⑦

PH

Walham

Gloucester

B4215

A38

B4063

2cm = 1km
1.25 Inches = 1 Mile

WAINLODE CLIFF

The Severn has bitten deep into the vulnerable marl of Wainlode Hill to form an almost sheer cliff rising abruptly from the water's edge. A number of old barges have been sunk at the base of the cliff in an attempt to prevent further erosion. The posts in the river here are to warn boatmen to keep to the other side of the channel, away from the cliff.

Leave the road just beyond the Red Lion, branching right to a stile and gate to climb above Wainlode Cliff into a large pasture. Keep right, heading upfield to a stile in a corner at the edge of woodland. Beyond the stile, go forward into a field for a few strides and then cross a stile on the right to enter the woodland. This is Norton Hill, which lies adjacent to Wainlode Hill. Just to the south, and worth the short detour, is Sandhurst Hill ❶, with excellent views out of all proportion to its modest height.

The Severn Way takes you through the woodland before crossing a flower meadow and then descending by steps through more woodland to rejoin the riverbank. When you leave the trees follow a right-hand field edge.

The continuing route now largely follows the edge of pasture, parallel with the course of the river. On the far bank is Ashleworth Ham ❷, a Gloucestershire Wildlife Trust nature reserve renowned for the number and variety of birds it attracts, especially wildfowl. Good all year round, it can be magnificent in winter.

Eventually the Severn Way crosses Rodway Lane ❸, an ancient access to a former ferry crossing.

ASHLEWORTH

The ferry linked the east bank with Ashleworth on the west bank. A later village has grown up a short distance away, but the original village is based around Ashleworth Quay, where a group of 15th century buildings still survives, offering tantalising glimpses to walkers on the Severn Way, prevented from crossing by the demise of the ferry.

Ashleworth Court is a beautiful stone house, which dates from 1460. Close by is a tithe barn, also of stone, and still in working use, though owned by the National Trust. The house and barn were built for St Augustine's Abbey, at Bristol, which acquired the manor of Ashleworth in 1154. An interesting church with some herringbone masonry (evidence of Saxon workmanship)

completes the medieval group and there is a 19th century pub by the river.

Continuing south by the Severn you pass a stretch known as Long Reach and walk through the leafy confines of Sandhurst Nature Reserve ❹, another Gloucestershire Wildlife Trust site. The reserve consists of disused brick pits and osier beds, where a mixture of wet woodland and open water supports a rich variety of wildlife.

Brick pits are a familiar feature along the Severn between Stourport and Gloucester, the local clays being ideal for brick-making. These pits were excavated in the 19th century and worked until 1924 when they were planted with osiers for basket-making, fencing and thatching.

Just the other side of Sandhurst village is Wallsworth Hall, the home of Nature in Art ❺, a wonderful museum and art gallery dedicated to all forms of art inspired by nature (closed Mondays).

When you reach Upper Parting ❻ the river splits into two channels. The Severn Way follows the East Channel and continues close by the river. After walking round a large field, keep to the right of two electricity pylons to locate a footbridge. The path steers you out towards a road. Turn right just before reaching it, cross a sluice gate, turn right to rejoin the riverbank and soon pass behind the Globe Inn and Restaurant ❼.

Yellow flag iris

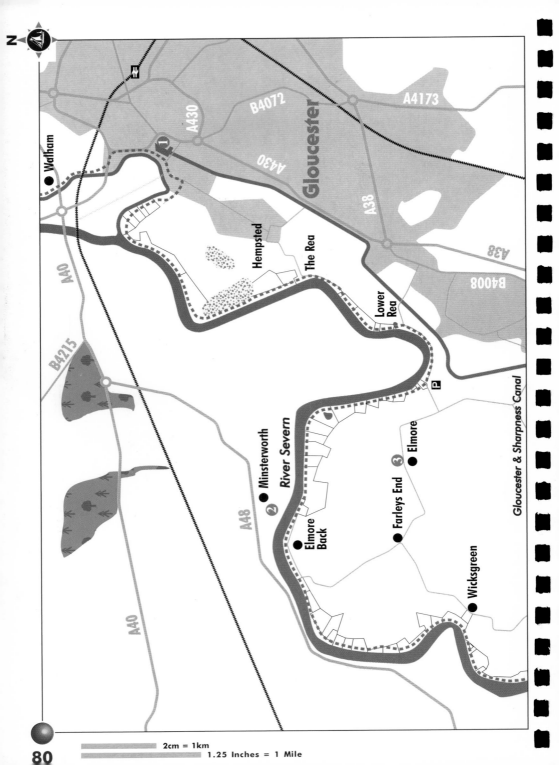

N

Walham

Gloucester

A430

B4072

A4173

A430

A38

A38

B4008

①

Hempsted

The Rea

Lower Rea

P

B4215

A40

Minsterworth

River Severn

②

Elmore Back

Farleys End

Elmore

③

A48

A40

Wicksgreen

Gloucester & Sharpness Canal

2cm = 1km

1.25 Inches = 1 Mile

The path leads on to the Jolly Waterman (a private house, no longer a pub), near the former Walham boatyard. Go down steps, and past some ponds, then on along the towpath as it passes beneath the A40 bypass bridge. Skirt a field and shortly pass under a railway viaduct to enter Westgate Park. Walk to the far side then turn right, under a fly-over, and proceed across the end of a pedestrian walkway and under another fly-over. Turn left to emerge at the roadside near a petrol station. Go past the garage, following the road round to meet Gloucester's Victorian quayside.

THE OLD QUAY

As with all the Severnside towns, Gloucester owed much of its early prosperity to its location on the river, although it was 1580 before a Royal Charter granted it the status of a port. The old quay, along which you are walking, was busy with trows and barges until the early 20th century.

When you reach the entrance to Gloucester Docks ❶ at Severn Road, either turn right over a swing bridge (no footpath), or proceed into the Docks and turn right over a lock gate, opposite the Antiques Centre. Turn right and walk around the building to rejoin Severn Road.

LLANTHONY PRIORY

At Llanthony Road turn right onto Hempsted Lane, soon passing the ruins of Llanthony Secunda Priory, an Augustinian house consecrated in 1136 after the original Llanthony Priory in the Black Mountains was attacked by Welsh raiders. Llanthony Secunda became highly prosperous, thanks to patronage from wealthy Gloucester families.

Turn right into Sudmeadow Road and, after the last terraced house on the right, turn right down a fenced path. At its end turn left to re-emerge beside the Severn, continuing along a riverside path that loops around Sud Meadow. With only a few minor deviations the on-going path now follows floodbanks almost all the way to Upper Framilode, ensuring easy and enjoyable walking beside the serpentine coils of the river.

Eventually, having passed the village of Hempsted, and approaching The Rea, branch left, still on an embankment, to a stile concealed in an overgrown hedge, beyond which you cross a footbridge to a road. Turn right and follow the road to its end, then, just before the last house, turn right through a gate and a garden to a stile, beyond which you rejoin the riverbank.

When you meet a road again at Lower Rea, turn right. Stay on the road for about 800m/yds, and then, as it bends left towards Elmore, leave it for a path returning to the riverbank. Continue past houses and then to a stile from which you set off through a series of riverside fields and orchards.

Elmore Back provides a fine view of Minsterworth Church ❷ across the river, and the wooded hills of the Forest of Dean are always in sight. The village of Elmore ❸ is set back from the Severn but is worth a detour if time allows: there are some fine houses, including Elmore Court, and the churchyard contains elaborately carved headstones and table tombs which are superb even by Gloucestershire standards.

Rarely now does the route leave the river or the adjacent floodbank, though along some stretches there is an alternative right of way that runs marginally closer to the Severn. Not far from Wicksgreen you leave the floodbank to go through an orchard at Waterend Farm. On the far side, go forward to a footbridge.

Tomb carving in the churchyard at Elmore

Gloucester Docks

THE city we now know as Gloucester stands close to the site chosen by the Roman army around AD50 when it was decided to build a fortress near the lowest safe crossing of the Severn. When the army moved on, Gloucester's urban life began and it received its first charter from Emperor Nerva (AD96-98) when it was granted the title of Colonia Nervia Glevensis - colonia being the highest status a Roman provincial town could attain. Glevum, as it was popularly known, never looked back. By the 10th century it was an important Saxon centre and the street plan of the present city centre owes as much to a rebuilding by Ethelfleda, daughter of Alfred the Great, as it does to the Romans.

During the reign of Edward the Confessor and his successor William the Conqueror, Gloucester was the regular meeting place of the King and Great Council, and its status was equalled only by Winchester and London. It was at Gloucester in 1085 that William ordered the survey that resulted in Domesday Book. In 1155, a charter of Henry I gave the town privileges equal to those of London and Westminster and Henry also granted Gloucester's citizens freedom of passage on the Severn. King John extended these privileges in 1200, and in 1216 Henry III was crowned at Gloucester, the only post-Conquest coronation not to take place at Westminster.

Throughout the succeeding centuries Gloucester continued to play a part in the nation's affairs, never more so than during the Civil War when it was the only Parliamentarian garrison between Bristol and the north-west. When peace was restored, Gloucester continued to grow and prosper, attaining over the centuries a diverse industrial and commercial base, which continues to this day. In recent years, tourism has become a significant element in the city's economy, largely due to the masterly refurbishment of Gloucester Docks.

Gloucester's most beautiful building is the Cathedral Church of St Peter and the Holy Trinity, which began life as the Abbey of St Peter, founded c680. It was rebuilt at least twice, but had fallen into decay by 1072 when King William appointed Serlo of Bayeux as its new Abbot. In 1089, Serlo embarked on a rebuilding programme which was to result in that masterpiece of the medieval stonemason's art which still dominates the city today. Serlo's cathedral was substantially complete by 1121, but a great period of rebuilding began in 1331, using the income from pilgrims to Edward II's tomb. Work began with the south transept, often regarded as the birthplace of Perpendicular architecture. Later additions include the magnificent tower, dating from 1450.

The Cathedral Close, known as College Green, has many lovely buildings, and there are several more on the fringes of the area. These are mostly tucked away in a network of winding streets and courtyards, and they need to be searched out. College Court is easily found, however, with its famous House of the Tailor of Gloucester, the setting for Beatrix Potter's eponymous story.

The other main attraction is Gloucester Docks, begun in 1794 and extended throughout the Victorian period. By the 1980s, waterborne commercial traffic had all but ceased and the huge dockside warehouses were no longer needed for storage. Most have since been renovated, and are now in use as offices, shops, bars and restaurants. One has become an antiques centre, while others accommodate museums, such as the enjoyable Robert Opie Collection at the Museum of Advertising and Packaging and the award-winning National Waterways Museum. The dock basins are now used mainly by leisure craft and boat trips are available. But working boatyards survive and, with the herring gulls screaming overhead, the atmosphere of a seaport lingers still.

Once you've seen the Docks and the Cathedral, it's easy to give up on Gloucester, which has, perhaps, been a victim of its own prosperity, continual redevelopment having destroyed most of its architectural heritage. Yet there is more to Gloucester than is first apparent. It has pleasant surprises round every corner and a visit to the Tourist Information Centre on Southgate Street is worthwhile. You can pick up a free map and then search out what remains of the old city.

One notable building, which is easily overlooked, is the New Inn on Northgate Street, built c1450 to accommodate pilgrims visiting the tomb of Edward II. The inn retains a rare medieval gallery built round a courtyard. On Southgate Street the Church of St Mary de Crypt is a good example of the Perpendicular style, while nearby Blackfriars, established in 1239, is the finest surviving Dominican friary in the country. There are many more fine buildings and several good museums, including the Folk Museum on Westgate Street, which has an excellent section on the River Severn.

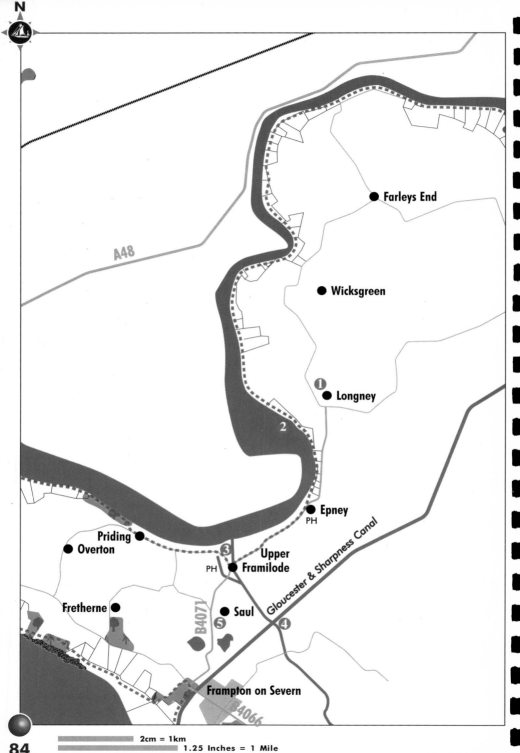

N

Farleys End

A48

Wicksgreen

1 Longney

2

Epney
PH

Priding
Overton

3
Upper
PH Framilode

Gloucester & Sharpness Canal

Fretherne

B4071

Saul

5

4

Frampton on Severn

B4066

2cm = 1km
1.25 Inches = 1 Mile

The Severn has been tidal since Gloucester and this short section from Wicksgreen sees it starting to widen as it approaches ever nearer to the sea. For some time, it has carved a deep and fast-flowing course, but now its pace slackens and at low tide mudflats and sandbanks appear, heralding the estuary to come and bringing a change of habitat for wildlife. Where once kingfishers darted and moorhens patrolled the river margins, now it's more likely that black-headed, lesser black-backed and herring gulls will be your companions.

There is no mistaking the route, which sticks faithfully to the riverside. The land on both sides of the Severn is flat, green and fertile; this used to be orchard country, with apples, pears and plums all flourishing in the rich soils, but most of the orchards have been grubbed out and replaced, mainly by dairy cattle, but also by sheep and cereals.

LONGNEY

As you pass the village of Longney the tower of 13th-century St Laurence's Church ❶ comes into view and it's worth the short detour (look out for a branching footpath) just to see the wonderfully carved 17th-, 18th- and 19th-century headstones in the churchyard. St Laurence's is beautifully positioned too, overlooking a large pond in which, on calm days, its reflection is ruffled only by a flotilla of contented-looking ducks.

The river, meanwhile, suddenly broadens dramatically to accommodate Longney Sands ❷, revealed in all their golden shimmer at low tide and often alive with a host of gulls and wading birds.

Approaching the end of the sands, you come to Bush Crib, where you pass a cottage and continue along the floodbank, crossing a section of cultivated turf to Longney Crib, where the Severn narrows again. It's just a short distance now to the hamlet of Epney, where the path comes out to a road at the Anchor Inn. Turn right and proceed to Upper Framilode, taking care against approaching traffic.

UPPER FRAMILODE

Architecturally, this is an unremarkable village, but it once had a certain commercial significance as the place where the now disused Stroudwater Navigation ❸ was joined to the Severn. The little River Frome also empties into the Severn at Framilode, and it is this waterway you cross as you approach a road junction. You will meet the Stroudwater further on as you turn right on the Severn Way, or you could make a slight detour to explore it further by branching left at the junction and continuing along the road until you come to Saul Bridge. A footpath follows the course of the Stroudwater to Saul Junction ❹ where it intersects the Gloucester and Sharpness Canal, and then on past Whitminster Church to Walk Bridge. This short diversion is recommended to anyone interested in our canal system, and Saul Junction is a pleasant place for a break. The Stroudwater Navigation is one of two disused canals which are often known as the Cotswold Canals. The Stroudwater was the first to be built, opening in 1779, and linking the Severn with the Cotswold mill town of Stroud. The Thames and Severn Canal was then constructed from Stroud to the River Thames at Lechlade, thus completing an important commercial link between our two greatest rivers.

The nearby village of Saul ❺ is also worth a visit, to see the idiosyncratic and colourfully painted carvings of subjects such as sailors and bargees which adorn several of the attractive 19th-century cottages.

Cuckoo flower - a once common spring meadow flower

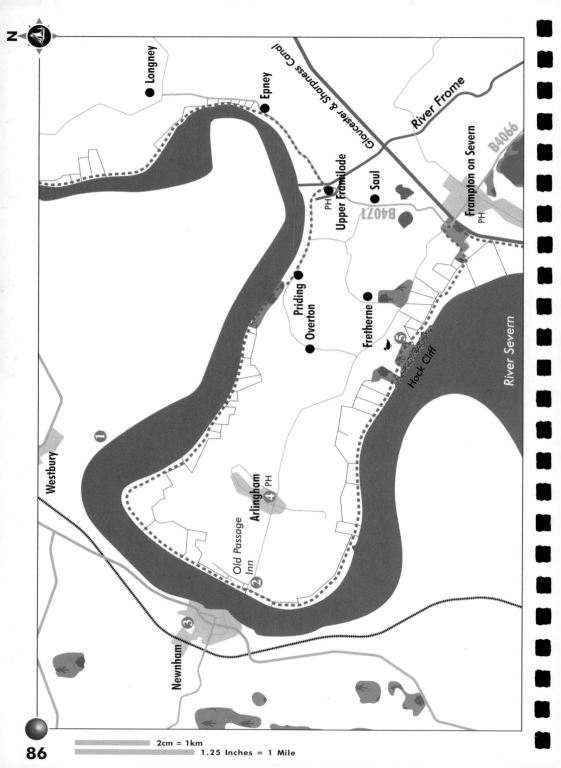

N

Longney

Epney

Gloucester & Sharpness Canal

River Frome

Frampton on Severn

B4066

Upper Framilode

PH

Saul

B4071

PH

Priding

Overton

Fretherne

River Severn

Hock Cliff

Westbury

Arlingham

PH

Old Passage Inn

Newnham

2cm = 1km

1.25 Inches = 1 Mile

ARLINGHAM PENINSULA

Walkers who, from a study of the map, realise that the shortest distance between Framilode and Frampton is little more than a mile, and so elect to shortcut this vast, sweeping loop, will be doing themselves a great disservice. Flood embankments, a widening river and a few small woodlands may not seem the most potent of ingredients, but this stretch should not be missed; it is a simple recipe, but as beautiful and relaxing as any part of the whole walk. And, in a stormy light, quite mesmeric.

Turn right at Upper Framilode, soon passing the Stroudwater Navigation, which used to join the Severn but now comes to an abrupt end by the road. Boatmen's cottages (and a pub) still stand, though extensively modernised. St Peter's Church is next, beside the Severn. Join a riverside path in front of the church and set off westward. The path leads to a gate and continues between fences before meeting a lane at Framilode. At a junction, bear right for Priding.

This stretch of the Severn was once much favoured by lamprey fishermen. The local name for the lamprey was 'pride', which is perpetuated in the name given to the hamlet of Priding. An ancient custom decreed that lampreys should be supplied to the king and that was the fate for many of those caught locally.

Just after Priding House, the road bends to the left. Leave it here to rejoin the riverside path. The route now follows the floodbank around the peninsula, with the spire of Westbury Church rising above the short escarpment of fossil-bearing Garden Cliff ❶ across the river, which is widening again now as the sandbanks become more extensive. In due course, you will arrive at the Old Passage Inn ❷.

THE OLD PASSAGE

There was a prehistoric river crossing here, connecting the Arlingham peninsula with the Forest of Dean iron mines. The Romans probably forded the river here (on elephant-back, it is said) before they established a new crossing at Gloucester. Cattle drovers continued to use the old crossing and a ferry also operated from the inn until comparatively recently. On the opposite bank is Newnham ❸, once a busy port, now a delightful small town with colour-washed houses and a cliff-top church overlooking the river.

The road from the inn leads to the village of Arlingham ❹, where there are some lovely old houses, a church with a superb collection of carved headstones and a tourist attraction in the form of St Augustine's Farm, a working farm open to the public.

The Severn Way continues along the floodbank. As you approach Hock Cliff ❺, which shows some interesting sedimentary layering rich in fossils, the path is diverted above it, through Smith's Wood and Long Wood, a nature reserve, before rejoining the floodbank.

When you reach a small in-flowing stream, Hock Ditch, leave the floodbank to head for a footbridge and then continue on a narrow path beyond, which gradually moves away from the river as you head towards Frampton on Severn. Keep forward and go round the edge of a wood, turning left along its boundary. Continue to a stile in a field corner and, beyond this, turn right on a path along the edge of a wood. Once over the next stile, near Saul Lodge, turn left along a field edge path. On meeting a road, turn right, then soon right again on the towpath of the Gloucester and Sharpness Canal.

Garden Cliff

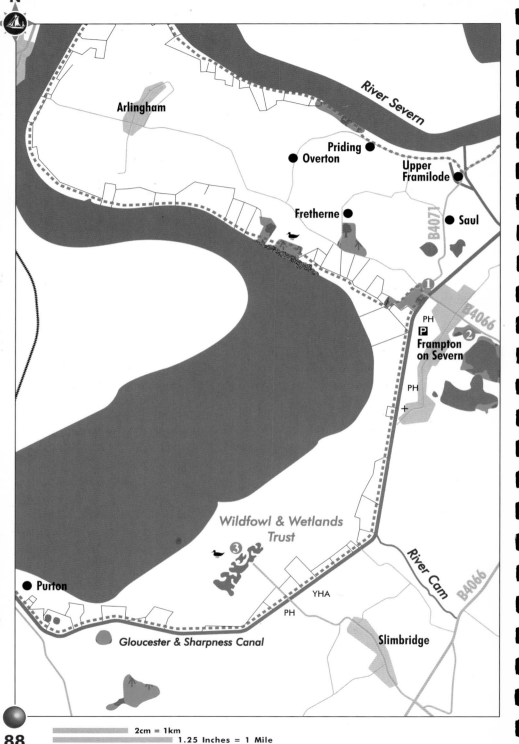

Arlingham

River Severn

Priding

Overton

Upper
Framilode

B4071

Fretherne

Saul

B4066

1

PH
P
Frampton
on Severn

2

PH

+

Wildfowl & Wetlands
Trust

3

River Cam

B4066

Purton

YHA

PH

Slimbridge

Gloucester & Sharpness Canal

2cm = 1km
1.25 Inches = 1 Mile

Between Frampton and Slimbridge, the route simply follows the towpath of the Gloucester and Sharpness Canal, giving the easiest of walking. As you join the towpath near Fretherne Bridge notice the bridgekeeper's house ❶, built in classical style with fluted Doric columns.

RAMPTON ON SEVERN

As the Severn Way heads resolutely south it bypasses Frampton, one of Gloucestershire's loveliest villages. A short detour into the village is warmly recommended (shops and pubs provide a further incentive). You can return to the towpath at Fretherne Bridge or walk the length of Frampton and rejoin the towpath at Splatt Bridge, near St Mary's Church.

Frampton is crammed with gorgeous old houses, many of which border Rosamund's Green, one of the largest village greens in the country. Grazed by ponies and geese, it is enhanced by three reedy ponds with resident ducks. Overlooking it is Manor Farm, where Henry II's mistress, Jane Clifford, is said to have been born. Henry's name for her was Rosamund ("rose of the world"), hence Rosamund's Green. A pair of mute swans, known to the villagers as Rosamund and Henry, raises a family each year by one of the ponds on the green.

Close by is Frampton Court ❷, a splendid Palladian-style mansion completed in 1733. The grounds include an ornamental canal and a Gothic orangery considered to be one of the finest garden buildings in the country. Between 1828 and 1851, eight female members of the Clifford family, living at Frampton Court, produced hundreds of watercolours of local wild flowers. For years the paintings lay forgotten in an attic until they were rediscovered and published in book form in 1985 as "The Frampton Flora", with a text by Richard Mabey.

At the southern end of the village is St Mary's Church, consecrated in 1315 and containing memorials to members of the Clifford family, though not to Henry's beloved Rosamund, who was buried at Godstow near Oxford in 1177 after being poisoned by Queen Eleanor.

By Splatt Bridge, to the south of the church, stands another classical-style canal cottage. As you head south on the towpath, the Severn is visible to the west, snaking through extensive sandbanks beyond low-lying saltmarsh grazed by horses and wildfowl.

Before long, just before reaching Cambridge Arms Bridge, you'll pass the unnavigable Cambridge Arm, which feeds the canal with water from the Cotswold escarpment. A little further south is Shepherd's Patch, where shepherds used to watch over flocks grazing by the river. There is a pub and a youth hostel here, also Patch Bridge, which carries Newgrounds Lane over the canal, linking Slimbridge village to Slimbridge Wildfowl and Wetlands Trust ❸.

LIMBRIDGE

This is home to the world's largest collection of captive wildfowl, living on pools in pens and paddocks. More importantly, it also encompasses extensive areas of mud, marsh and meadow, forming a vital wildfowl sanctuary. Well-placed hides enable visitors to see some of the wild birds attracted to these rich feeding grounds.

The Wildfowl and Wetlands Trust (WWT) was founded in 1946 (as the Wildfowl Trust) by the late Sir Peter Scott, a great painter and naturalist. His aim was 'to establish a centre for the scientific study, public display and conservation of the wildfowl of the world'.

Slimbridge

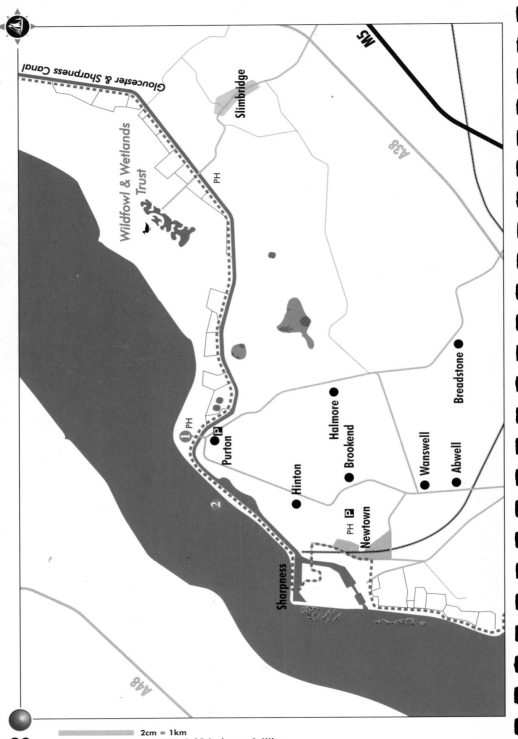

N

Gloucester & Sharpness Canal

Slimbridge

M5

A38

Wildfowl & Wetlands Trust

PH

Breadstone

Halmore

PH
Purton
P

Brookend

Hinton

Wanswell

Abwell

2

Newtown
PH P

Sharpness

A48

2cm = 1km
1.25 Inches = 1 Mile

GLOUCESTER & SHARPNESS CANAL

Beyond the turning for Slimbridge, the Severn Way, now heading in a westerly direction, simply continues along the canal towpath. The Gloucester and Sharpness Canal began life in 1794 as the Gloucester and Berkeley Canal. Construction work was dogged by a series of problems and was temporarily abandoned in 1800 when funds ran out. Work resumed in 1817 under the supervision of Thomas Telford who decided to terminate the canal at Sharpness instead. Even so, it wasn't until 1827 that it was finally completed. It was, at that time, the widest and deepest ship canal in the world. In bypassing the shifting sands of the treacherous Severn it facilitated the passage of large ships to Gloucester and led to a considerable expansion of the city's trade.

The towpath reaches the little village of Purton ❶ where there is another neo-classical bridgekeeper's cottage, and where the canal loops round, heading first north, then south. Until very recently, there were two pubs at Purton; one of them, the Berkeley Hunt Inn, was scarcely distinguishable from a farmhouse and was renowned for its completely unspoilt atmosphere. Sadly, it is now a private house. The other pub, The Berkeley Arms, still survives, occupying a pleasant riverside site.

Continuing along the towpath, you find yourself walking on a narrow spit of land squeezed between canal and river, with Waveridge Sand and Ridge Sand ❷ exposed at low tide. The rotting hulks of old barges have been beached along the reed-fringed shore in an effort to prevent erosion, their presence adding to the melancholic but strangely captivating atmosphere which prevails in certain weather conditions.

As you approach Sharpness you pass a circular stone abutment which once supported a railway swing bridge spanning the canal. There was also an adjoining rail bridge across the Severn, built in 1879 but badly damaged by two out-of-control tanker barges in 1960. The bridge was later demolished.

SHARPNESS

Something of a surprise in rural Gloucestershire, Sharpness Docks mark the southern terminus of the canal. The Old Dock, designed by Telford, was soon considered too small to cope with the larger ships and growing volume of trade that the canal generated and so a New Dock was constructed in 1874. Today, it is still a busy port, where containers are transhipped onto lorries. The old tidal basin is disused now but the arm leading to it serves as a marina.

On reaching the marina, proceed to the far end, cross a footbridge, turn up a flight of steps to a private car park and walk out on an access lane. Follow it down to a road junction and turn left. Walk towards a T-junction ahead, but take the first turning on the left and follow this to the more northerly of two bridges and onto a surfaced lane. Follow the lane as it bends right, just in front of the Severn View Nursing Home, and head towards the rows of houses that form part of Newtown.

Pass the Pier View Hotel and, a little further on, leave the road, turning right onto a path between a fence and hedgerow. At the end of the path, cross a railway line and keep on in the same direction until you can turn right to a main road. At the road, turn right and go down to a crossroads then turn left. When you reach a row of terraced cottages go forward past the gable-end to rejoin the River Severn, turning left.

River Severn at Sharpness

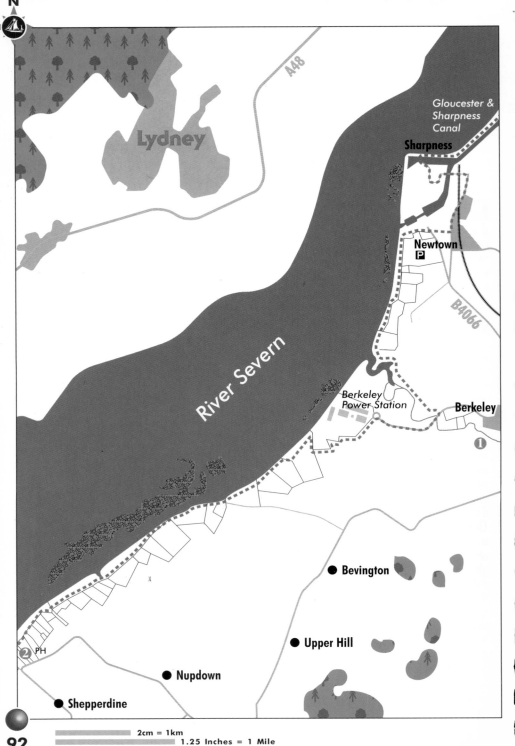

N

Lydney

A48

Gloucester &
Sharpness
Canal

Sharpness

Newtown
P

B4066

River Severn

Berkeley
Power Station

Berkeley

1

Bevington

Upper Hill

2 PH

Nupdown

Shepperdine

2cm = 1km
1.25 Inches = 1 Mile

Having regained the riverside flood embankment south of Sharpness Docks, walk along it until you meet Berkeley Pill, an in-flowing creek. Turn left here, and go through a metal gate, continuing on a floodbank until it ends near another gate. Initially, keep forward alongside the creek, but then strike across the next field towards a distant warehouse. Aim to the right of it to locate a stile, and then go behind the warehouse to a road bridge. The Severn Way now turns right but you may first wish to visit Berkeley, which lies to the left.

BERKELEY

There is a range of services here (shops, pubs and accommodation) and much of historical interest. The town is Georgian in appearance, but of ancient foundation and renowned for its Norman castle ❶, which originated in 1067, was rebuilt in 1154, and substantially remodelled between 1340 and 1350. With its massive shell keep and pink and grey battlemented walls, it's one of the most spectacular castles in the country.

The manor was given by William I to Roger de Berkeley of Dursley, but de Berkeley's grandson chose the wrong side in the civil war of King Stephen's reign and his estates were granted to Robert FitzHarding, a wealthy Bristolian. FitzHarding rebuilt the castle in 1154, his son and daughter diplomatically married into the Berkeley family and their descendants have lived there ever since. The castle has been visited by at least sixteen sovereigns and has witnessed many notable events, including the gathering in 1215 of the West Country barons before the signing of Magna Carta at Runnymede, the brutal murder of Edward II in 1327 and a siege by Oliver Cromwell in 1645.

Close to the castle is St Mary's Church, which contains the Berkeley tombs and has some fine table tombs in the churchyard, including that of Dicky Pearce, England's last court jester, who died in 1728. The church has an unusual detached belltower built in 1753. Overlooking the churchyard is the Jenner Museum, a handsome Georgian house dedicated to the work of Dr Edward Jenner, the Berkeley man who in 1796 developed a vaccine for smallpox.

Resuming the Severn Way, return to the bridge and follow the road towards Berkeley Power Station. As you approach the entrance, turn left to a kissing gate and go along the ensuing footpath to a footbridge, after which a fenced path shepherds you round the power station grounds to a gate from where you strike out across pasture towards the river. Go through two gates and forward onto a concrete breakwater, where you overlook the Severn once more.

The route now simply follows the river, with the golden sands of Lydney dominating the far shore. Soon after passing Severn House Farm you leave Gloucestershire for the new authority of South Gloucestershire (previously Avon, and, before that, Gloucestershire). After passing the attractive White House, a lightkeeper's home, you come to Chapel House, originally a 14th-century chapel, whose priest doubled as lightkeeper. Beyond this, you reach the Windbound Inn ❷ at Shepperdine.

SHEPPERDINE

This is a scattered settlement whose inn has the distinction of being exactly 200 miles (320km) from the source of the Severn. It is also the place where the Severn Way, in its earliest incarnation, came to an end, just 50 miles (80km) from its Tewkesbury starting point.

Headstone at St Mary's Church

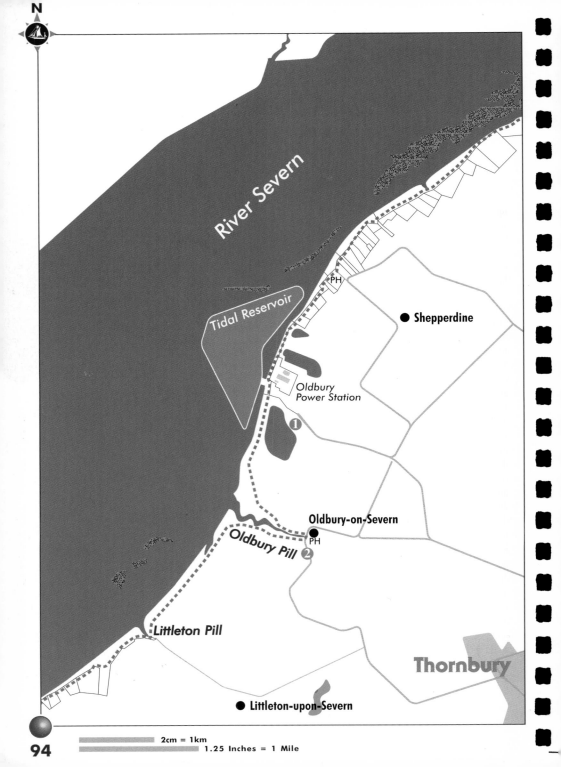

N

River Severn

Tidal Reservoir

PH

● **Shepperdine**

Oldbury
Power Station

①

● **Oldbury-on-Severn**
PH

②

Oldbury Pill

Littleton Pill

● **Littleton-upon-Severn**

Thornbury

2cm = 1km
1.25 Inches = 1 Mile

After the Windbound Inn the route simply follows the shore of the estuary, heading initially for Oldbury Power Station. The two southernmost and largest of all the 100 Severn bridges are now in view, still some distance away, but indicating that the end of this outstanding journey is in sight.

OLDBURY POWER STATION

The estuary is home to a wide variety of birdlife and is especially popular with over-wintering birds like white-fronted geese. Ugly, and perhaps menacing, though it is, the nuclear power station is not necessarily detrimental to wildlife. In fact, its lagoon and reservoir are much frequented by waders and the building itself is sometimes used as a perch by peregrine falcons.

The power station has been in operation since 1967. When running at full power its twin reactors produce enough electricity to supply a city one-and-a-half times the size of Bristol. Most power stations are situated either on the coast or adjacent to substantial rivers because they require large quantities of cooling water to condense the steam from the turbines. Oldbury requires approximately 70 million litres of water an hour, and to ensure that this supply is maintained a large tidal reservoir has been constructed offshore.

Just as you approach the power station you pass a silt lagoon ❶, adjacent to a nature trail which explores meadows, an orchard, woodland and some small ponds. The lagoon attracts significant numbers of shore birds, especially waders, because it provides ideal conditions for them at high tide, when they require roosting sites which have good all round vision and are free from disturbance. Dunlin, curlew and redshank are the main species here throughout the year, but migrant waders in spring and autumn may include ringed plover, sanderling, whimbrel, bar-tailed godwit, sandpiper and stint. At low water the waders are spread out thinly over the mudflats, though turnstones feed mainly on the rocks close to shore.

Excavation of the power station lagoon in 1992 revealed remains of a Romano-British settlement in occupation between the 2nd and 4th centuries AD. Archaeologists uncovered a wealth of material, suggesting that the area was more intensively settled than was previously thought.

Continuing south from the power station, you reach Oldbury Pill, where a small yacht club is based. Turn inland along the on-going embankment, shortly joining a surfaced track. Keep on along this until you come into Oldbury-on-Severn at a T-junction.

OLDBURY-ON-SEVERN

The village, with its pleasant cottages and welcoming inn, is overlooked by the remains of an Iron Age hillfort called The Toot and by St Arilda's Church ❷, standing on a knoll to the south.

Turn right and go past the Anchor Inn. After 100m/yds, turn right at the Oldbury Equestrian Centre. Follow a track past stables and then cross a paddock to a stile, beyond which you go forward to rejoin the sea wall by the mouth of Oldbury Pill. At low water, the vast expanse of Oldbury Sands is exposed, as well as the unattractively named Slimeroad Sand bordering the main river channel - Slime Road - beyond which lies Sedbury Cliff, where Offa's Dyke Path begins its northward journey through the Marches.

As you reach Littleton Pill the route is deflected inland again. Remain on the embankment, heading for a stile beside a gate, and then continue along the sea wall above Littleton Warth.

Bugle - a wet meadow and woodland plant

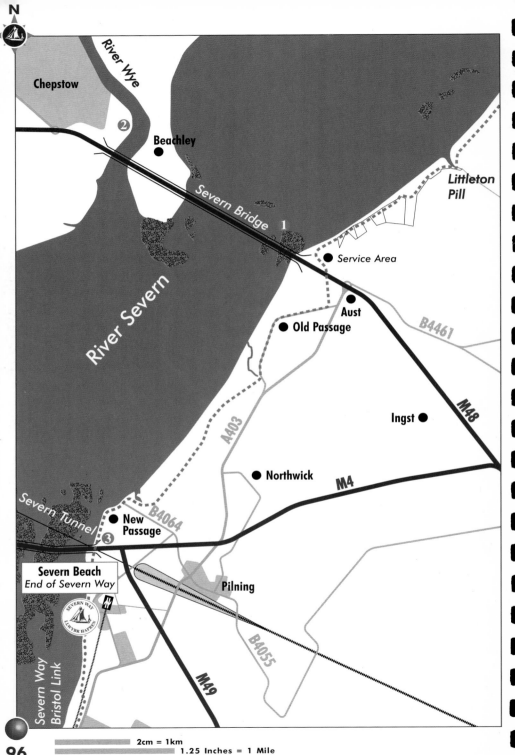

N

Chepstow

River Wye

Beachley

Severn Bridge

1

Littleton Pill

River Severn

Service Area

Aust

Old Passage

B4461

A403

M48

Ingst

Northwick

M4

Severn Tunnel

New Passage

B4064

3

Severn Beach
End of Severn Way

SEVERN WAY
LLWYBR HAFREN

Pilning

B4055

Severn Way
Bristol Link

M49

2cm = 1km

1.25 Inches = 1 Mile

Once past Littleton Pill keep on along the shoreline until you draw level with an electricity sub-station. Here a track turns in from the shore, and a stile gives access to a large sloping pasture. Climb up the right-hand edge of this to a dilapidated look-out at the top. Keep forward along the edge of two more fields beside a hedge, gaps in which reveal a sheer cliff, to be approached only with great caution. A stile gives access to the grounds of the Severn View Service Area overlooking the Severn Bridge ❶ at Aust. Proceed to a viewing area, and follow a path round the perimeter of the service area until you can cross the motorway (M48) on a footbridge.

OLD PASSAGE

The name Aust may derive either from "trajectus augusti", a Roman route which crossed the Severn, or from St Augustine, who is believed by some authorities to have met with the Welsh bishops here. The river crossing is traditionally known as Old Passage and a ferry service operated until Severn Bridge opened in 1966. The bridge, which can be walked or cycled across, is a remarkable feat of engineering, spanning the Severn between Aust Rock and Beachley, then continuing across the River Wye ❷ to enter Wales near Chepstow, providing walkers with a link to Offa's Dyke Path and the Wye Valley Walk.

Just south of the bridge the Wye, having taken a more direct route from Plynlimon, joins the Severn, and the combined flow, soon augmented by the Usk and the Avon, moves smoothly on towards the Bristol Channel and the Atlantic.

Having crossed the motorway, bear left and continue to a junction about 100m/yds away from the A403. Ignore the A-road, and turn right along a quiet lane that goes through Old Passage, soon passing, on the left, St Augustine's Vineyard, another indication that the saint may have come this way.

Just after crossing Cake Pill, not far from the A403, turn right through a kissing gate and walk along an embankment, following this into a military firing range, marked on maps as a danger area. When red flags are flying there is no admission, but an alternative route is available on rights of way around the perimeter. This is due to a 1934 War Department Bylaw which restricts access during times of firing.

On the other side of the firing range, cross a creek (The Pill) and turn right on a track to pass Red Lodge and Severn Lodge Farm, now following a surfaced lane beside the estuary. Keep forward to pass beneath the Second Severn Crossing ❸

NEW PASSAGE

Opened in 1996, the newest of all the Severn bridges is Britain's longest river crossing, and was built at a cost of £330,000,000. It carries the M4 and rests partly on a large rock outcrop, English Stones, reducing the need for special foundations. As you pass under the bridge, you will find a visitor centre, opened in late 1998, just off to the left, with information about the Severn crossings.

Now simply keep forward on a concrete walkway (the Binn Wall) to reach Severn Beach and the end of the Severn Way. If you now look across to Monmouthshire, you will see that the river that began as a mere trickle on the moorland heights of Plynlimon has grown to be more than 6km (almost 4 miles) wide.

Severn Beach has shops, cafés and pubs, as well as buses and trains to Bristol. Public transport provides the obvious link to the city, but walkers with enough energy, and another day to spare, should consider continuing along the Bristol Link, which leads from Severn Beach into the heart of Bristol.

Severn Beach

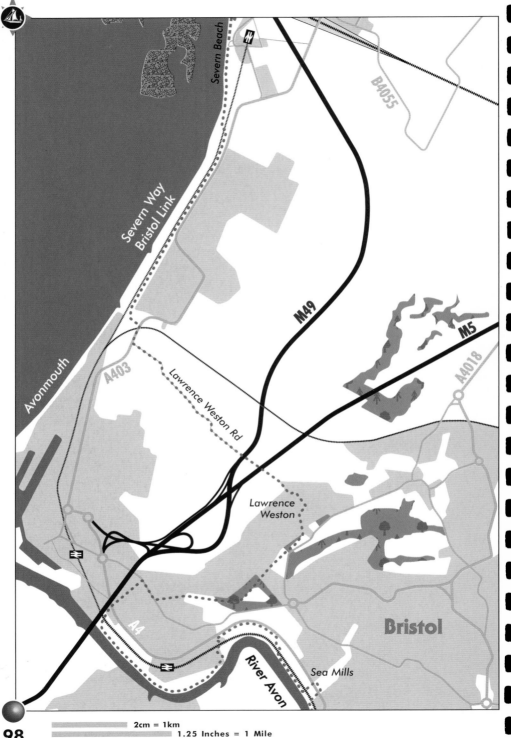

N

Severn Beach

B4055

Severn Way
Bristol Link

M49

M5

Avonmouth

A403

Lawrence Weston Rd

A4018

Lawrence
Weston

Bristol

A4

River Avon

Sea Mills

2cm = 1km
1.25 Inches = 1 Mile

From Severn Beach go forward along the concrete pathway that continues beside the estuary from the end of the breakwater. Gradually the pathway deteriorates into a cinder track and goes through scrub to parallel the course of the railway. Stay beside the railway to a crossing point, cross with care and then follow a path to the A403. The A-road is busy, so the route makes use of a path cut through a reed bed in Chittening Warth, parallel with the road. From time to time, the route pops out onto the road, but soon returns to the safer line.

Where the A403 makes a sharp left bend, the link route touches on the bend, but maintains its original direction. Before long you cross a large black pipeline and bear right through scrubland, soon with a fern-filled rhine to your left. As the scrub thins out you can see the Severn again, and, less welcome perhaps, the smokestacks of Newport on the far side. After this, the path bears left towards a railway junction at Hallen Marsh. Cross two railway lines, with great care, to reach a surfaced path and turn left to rejoin the A403.

At the road, turn right and walk to the roundabout at the edge of Cabot Park (an industrial estate). Turn left onto Lawrence Weston Road, which soon leaves the industrial buildings behind and becomes an attractive country lane flanked by reed beds and rhines. It eventually passes beneath the M49 and then goes over the M5 before reaching the edge of Lawrence Weston, a suburb of Bristol.

Turn right, still on Lawrence Weston Road and go up to a road junction (Long Cross). Turn left and take the first right, still Lawrence Weston Road. Go straight on at a crossroads then turn right into Broadlands Drive. About 130m/yds after the turning take a footpath on the left down steps. The path soon climbs uphill between wooded banks, and then, as it levels out, swings to the right.

Immediately after passing an area of grassland, turn right into woodland, and then left along its edge, climbing slightly. You come to a stile into a field: don't cross it, but turn right and follow a fence round to a waymarked post where you turn right through woodland, shortly climbing steps.

The path starts to descend, and is quite steep and slippery in places. Reaching a waymarked post turn left, climbing gently uphill and aiming for another post above. When you reach it, turn right and ascend to the edge of a large field. Soon the path forks, and you branch right to follow it round the field edge to a junction. Go down to meet a surfaced path that leads out to a road, not far from the Penpole Inn.

Cross the road and go into the woodland of Shirehampton opposite, immediately turning right. As the path climbs, the view opens out to include a large stone mansion, Kingsweston House, just above the path. Climb to a large field where the Bristol Link turns right past sycamores and then along an avenue of mature lime trees. At a waymarked junction fork right, and at the next junction fork left, walking through mixed woodland, alive with squirrels and jays.

At the next junction, keep forward on the main path. At the next, branch left, then soon fork right, still walking through mixed woodland. When you reach a clearing, go straight across on a well-trodden path, walking now along the narrow ridge-top to a trig point. Keep forward, soon descending steps to Penpole Lane. Proceed to a T-junction, and turn right into Lower High Street.

Go straight on at traffic lights (past the Hope and Anchor pub), and soon turn left into West Town Road. At the end of the road, where you are immediately beneath the M5 motorway, go to the main road ahead, cross with care and turn right to the Avon Riverside Trading Estate. Pass under the motorway again, and immediately left onto a pathway that finds a way round a road engineer's compound before doubling back to join an old surfaced road.

The path stays close to the River Avon for a while, and then wends its way inland through scrub before joining an old road, at which point you continue in the same direction to reach the Lamplighters pub. Pass in front of it and on along the right-hand edge of playing fields. Across the river is the village of Pill, to which a ferry used to operate.

Eventually you come to the edge of a housing estate. Keep on in the same direction until a padlocked gate prevents further progress alongside the river. Turn left into Riverside Close. At a T-junction, turn right, climbing to cross a railway bridge, and walk out to the A4. Turn right for a little over 1km (half a mile) to a viewing point. Leave the road here, on the right, for a path descending through woods and a meadow to a playing field.

Cross the field to a railway bridge, and on the other side bear left to rejoin the banks of the Avon. A well-trodden path leads eventually to where the River Trym flows into the Avon at Sea Mills. Turn left under rail and road bridges, then cross a footbridge and turn right again down Sea Mills Lane, back underneath the road bridge and forward to Sea Mills Station.

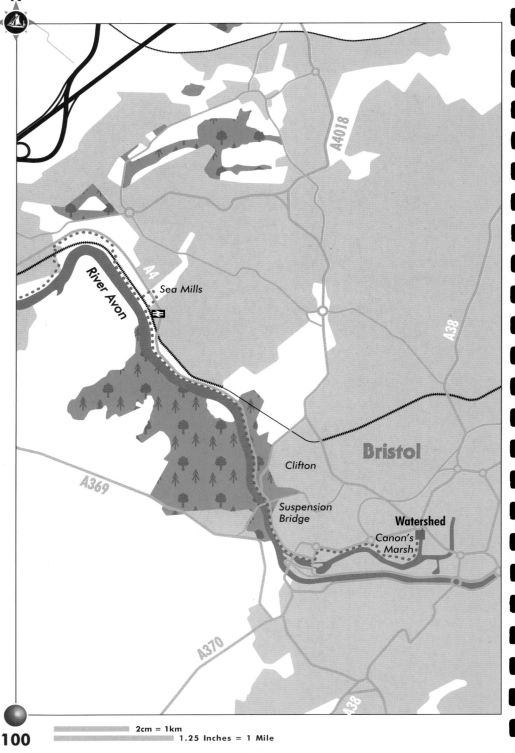

N

River Avon

A4

A4018

A38

Sea Mills

Bristol

Clifton

A369

Suspension
Bridge

Watershed

Canon's
Marsh

A38

A370

2cm = 1km
1.25 Inches = 1 Mile

Go past Sea Mills Station and head towards the Avon again, turning left by an old signal station on a very pleasant path above the river. As the path moves slightly away from the Avon there are steps up to the road. Don't be diverted up here, stay by the edge of the trees above the river. Soon the beautiful wooded cliffs of the Avon Gorge National Nature Reserve begin to make their presence felt ahead.

The path eventually leads through woodland to a flight of steps leading up to the A4. Turn right and follow the road as it heads for Bristol, but take care because the pedestrian walkway is also a cycleway. Once you have passed beneath the magnificent suspension bridge you soon move down onto the quayside and go forward past locks as you approach Bristol's floating harbour. Pass under a road bridge, and then go alongside a dock basin to another bridge. Go up to the bridge and turn left, crossing the road near the Pumphouse. Walk along Merchants Road, turning right at the end of it.

Keep on along a road until, just past Michael's Restaurant, where the roadside footpath ends, you can turn right at Mardyke Steps. Turn left along Mardyke Wharf, and shortly pass the SS Great Britain. At the end of the wharf, return to a roadside footpath. At a major junction bear right, following the road into Canon's Marsh, beyond which is the Watershed Centre and the end of the Bristol Link.

For a slightly better finish, leave the road not long after the major junction, by turning right onto a cobbled lane between high walls. This takes you back to the floating harbour. You then simply follow the quayside through Hannover Quay and round to reach the Watershed.

Clifton Suspension Bridge

FOR UP-TO-DATE INFORMATION ON TRANSPORT AND ACCOMMODATION, PLEASE CONTACT THE LOCAL TIC.

TOURIST INFORMATION CENTRES

POWYS
LLANIDLOES
The Town Hall, Llanidloes
Tel 01686 412605
NEWTOWN
Central Car Park, Newtown
Tel 01686 6255580
WELSHPOOL
Vicarage Gardens, Car Park, Welshpool
Tel 01938 552043

SHROPSHIRE
SHREWSBURY
Music Hall, The Square, Shrewsbury
Tel 01743 350761
IRONBRIDGE
The Wharfage, Ironbridge
Tel 01952 432166
BRIDGNORTH
The Library, Listley Street, Bridgnorth
Tel 01746 763257

WORCESTERSHIRE
BEWDLEY
Load Street, Bewdley
Tel 01299 404 740
WORCESTER
The Guildhall, High Street, Worcester
Tel 01905 726311
UPTON UPON SEVERN
4 High Street, Upton upon Severn
Tel 01684 594200

GLOUCESTERSHIRE & SOUTH GLOUCESTERSHIRE
TEWKESBURY
Tewkesbury Museum, 64 Barton Street, Tewkesbury
Tel 01684 295027
GLOUCESTER
28 Southgate Street, Gloucester
Tel 01452 421188
THORNBURY
Town Hall, High Street, Thornbury
Tel 01454 281638

BRISTOL
BRISTOL
The Bristol Tourism and Conference Bureau, St Nicholas Church, St Nicholas Street, Bristol
Tel 0117 9260767

TRANSPORT

BY TRAIN
NATIONAL TRAIN HELPLINE
TEL 0345 484950
SEVERN VALLEY RAILWAY
ENQUIRIES 01299 403816

BY BUS
POWYS
TEL 01597 826642 - 826678
SHROPSHIRE
TEL 0345 056785
WORCESTERSHIRE
TEL 0345 125436
GLOUCESTERSHIRE
TEL 01452 425543
SOUTH GLOUCESTERSHIRE & BRISTOL
TEL 0117 9555111

BY COACH
NATIONAL EXPRESS
TEL 0990 808080

COUNCIL PHONE NOs

POWYS
**Planning, Economic Development and Regeneration.
Public Rights of Way**
Tel 01597 826583
SHROPSHIRE
**Countryside Service.
Rights of Way Access Section Officer**
Tel 01743 255054
WORCESTERSHIRE
Countryside Service
Tel 01905 766493
GLOUCESTERSHIRE
Public Rights of Way
Tel 01452 425577
SOUTH GLOUCESTERSHIRE
Public Rights of Way
Tel 01454 868686
BRISTOL
**Traffic and Transport Planning.
Public Rights of Way**
Tel 0117 9036890

TO REPORT POLLUTION, FISH IN DISTRESS AND FOR INFORMATION ON FLOODING IN THE SEVERN CATCHMENT AND THE SEVERN BORE, RING THE ENVIRONMENT AGENCY ON: SHREWSBURY 01743 272828 OR TEWKESBURY 01684 850951